# CGP has autumn term Maths conkered!

Ah, autumn. The season of mists, mellow fruitfulness and Maths practice. And if you're looking for Maths, you've come to the right place...

This brilliant CGP book gathers a huge range of skills from the Year 5 curriculum — there's a page of practice for every day of the autumn term.

It's perfect for use in class or at home, with plenty of examples and colourful pictures to keep pupils interested. It's not to be mist!

# What CGP is all about

Our sole aim here at CGP is to produce the highest quality books — carefully written, immaculately presented and dangerously close to being funny.

Then we work our socks off to get them out to you — at the cheapest possible prices.

# Contents

☑ Use the tick boxes to help keep a record of which tests have been attempted.

## Week 1
- ☑ Day 1 .................... 1
- ☑ Day 2 .................... 2
- ☑ Day 3 .................... 3
- ☑ Day 4 .................... 4
- ☑ Day 5 .................... 5

## Week 2
- ☑ Day 1 .................... 6
- ☑ Day 2 .................... 7
- ☑ Day 3 .................... 8
- ☑ Day 4 .................... 9
- ☑ Day 5 .................... 10

## Week 3
- ☑ Day 1 .................... 11
- ☑ Day 2 .................... 12
- ☑ Day 3 .................... 13
- ☑ Day 4 .................... 14
- ☑ Day 5 .................... 15

## Week 4
- ☑ Day 1 .................... 16
- ☑ Day 2 .................... 17
- ☑ Day 3 .................... 18
- ☑ Day 4 .................... 19
- ☑ Day 5 .................... 20

## Week 5
- ☑ Day 1 .................... 21
- ☑ Day 2 .................... 22
- ☑ Day 3 .................... 23
- ☑ Day 4 .................... 24
- ☑ Day 5 .................... 25

## Week 6
- ☑ Day 1 .................... 26
- ☑ Day 2 .................... 27
- ☑ Day 3 .................... 28
- ☑ Day 4 .................... 29
- ☑ Day 5 .................... 30

## Week 7
- ☑ Day 1 .................... 31
- ☑ Day 2 .................... 32
- ☑ Day 3 .................... 33
- ☑ Day 4 .................... 34
- ☑ Day 5 .................... 35

## Week 8
- ☑ Day 1 .................... 36
- ☑ Day 2 .................... 37
- ☑ Day 3 .................... 38
- ☑ Day 4 .................... 39
- ☑ Day 5 .................... 40

## Week 9

- ☑ Day 1 .................... 41
- ☑ Day 2 .................... 42
- ☑ Day 3 .................... 43
- ☑ Day 4 .................... 44
- ☑ Day 5 .................... 45

## Week 10

- ☑ Day 1 .................... 46
- ☑ Day 2 .................... 47
- ☑ Day 3 .................... 48
- ☑ Day 4 .................... 49
- ☑ Day 5 .................... 50

## Week 11

- ☑ Day 1 .................... 51
- ☑ Day 2 .................... 52
- ☑ Day 3 .................... 53
- ☑ Day 4 .................... 54
- ☑ Day 5 .................... 55

## Week 12

- ☑ Day 1 .................... 56
- ☑ Day 2 .................... 57
- ☑ Day 3 .................... 58
- ☑ Day 4 .................... 59
- ☑ Day 5 .................... 60

Answers .................... 61

Published by CGP

ISBN: 978 1 78908 655 3

Editors: Katie Fernandez, Emily Forsberg, Paul Jordin, Duncan Lindsay, Claire Plowman, James Summersgill

With thanks to Alison Griffin and Rachael Rogers for the proofreading.

With thanks to Lottie Edwards for the copyright research.

Clipart from Corel®

Printed by Elanders Ltd, Newcastle upon Tyne.
Based on the classic CGP style created by Richard Parsons.

Text, design, layout and original illustrations© Coordination Group Publications Ltd. (CGP) 2020
All rights reserved.

Photocopying this book is not permitted, even if you have a CLA licence.
Extra copies are available from CGP with next day delivery • 0800 1712 712 • www.cgpbooks.co.uk

# How to Use this Book

- This book contains 60 daily practice tests.

- We've split them into 12 sections — that's roughly one for each week of the Year 5 autumn term.

- Each week is made up of 5 tests, so there's one for every school day of the term (Monday – Friday).

- Each test should take about 10 minutes to complete.

- The tests contain a mix of topics from Year 4 and Year 5 Maths. New Year 5 topics are gradually introduced as you go through the book.

- The tests increase in difficulty as you progress through the term.

- Each test looks something like this:

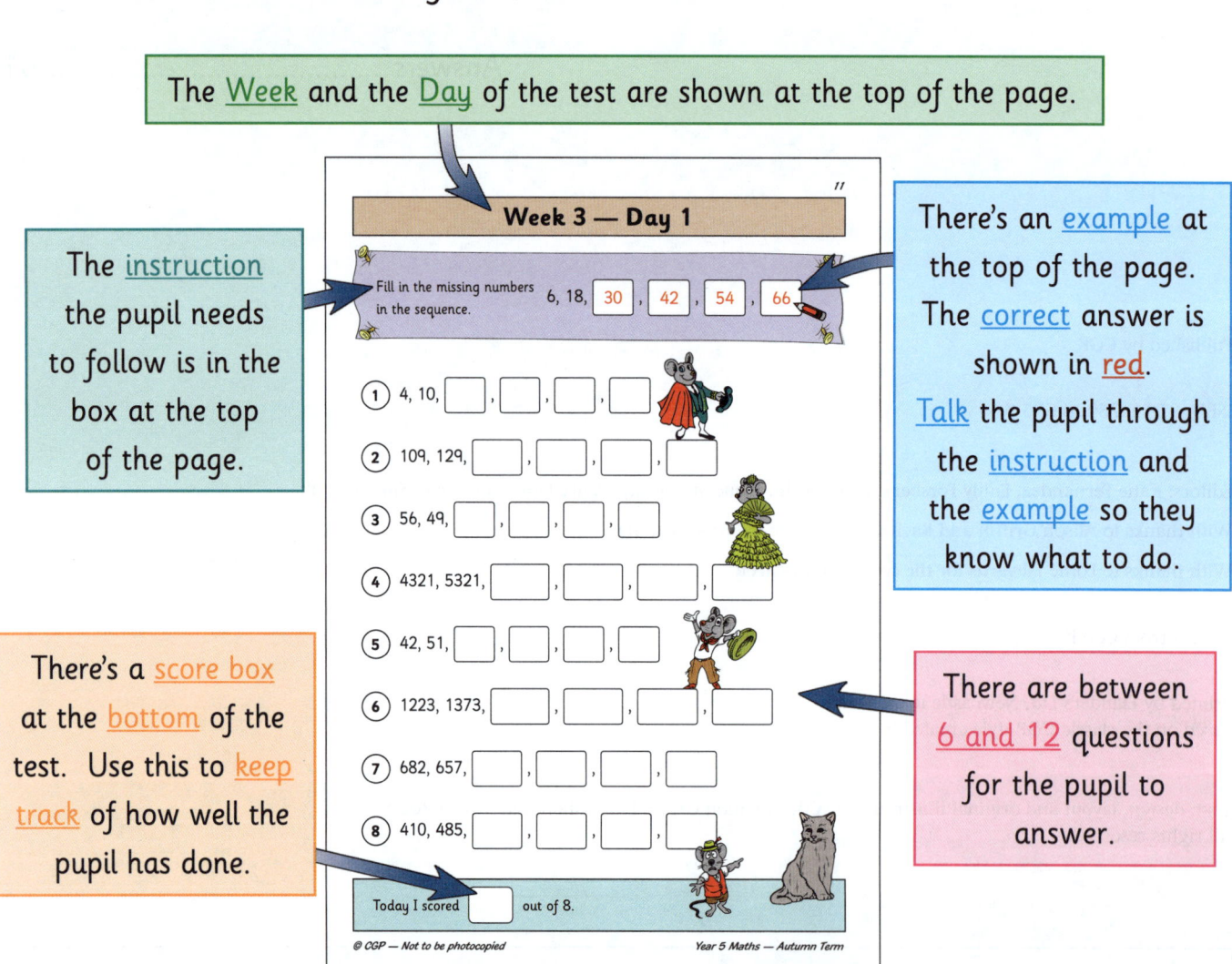

# Week 1 — Day 1

Fill in the answer.   37 + 100 = [ 137 ]

1) 89 + 100 =
2) 412 − 100 =
3) 285 + 100 =
4) 921 − 100 =
5) 159 + 100 =
6) 8263 − 1000 =
7) 5702 + 1000 =
8) 3192 − 1000 =
9) 6043 − 1000 =
10) 389 + 1000 =
11) 1235 + 100 =
12) 7389 − 100 =

Today I scored [ ] out of 12.

# Week 1 — Day 2

Draw an arrow on the number line to show roughly where the number is.

**1578**

← 1560 — 1570 — 1580 → (arrow above ~1578)

**1** 1331

← 1330 — 1340 — 1350 →

**2** 1643

← 1640 — 1660 — 1680 →

**3** 787

← 780 — 790 →

**4** 540

← 500 — 550 — 600 →

**5** 1911

← 1890 — 1900 — 1910 →

**6** 2519

← 2510 — 2515 — 2520 →

**7** 7008

← 7005 — 7010 — 7015 — 7020 →

**8** 2055

← 2025 — 2050 — 2075 →

Today I scored ☐ out of 8.

# Week 1 — Day 3

Circle the longest distance.

(1.2 m)    105 cm

1. 5.8 m    582 cm
2. 7.6 m    716 cm
3. 0.7 m    69 cm
4. 15.2 m    150 cm
5. 19 m    1801 cm
6. 23.2 m    2322 cm
7. 1.15 m    117 cm
8. 3.54 m    361 cm
9. 20.03 m    1998 cm
10. 11.09 m    1119 cm

Today I scored [ ] out of 10.

# Week 1 — Day 4

Draw the point on the grid.
Join the points to make a polygon.
Write down the name of the polygon you have drawn.

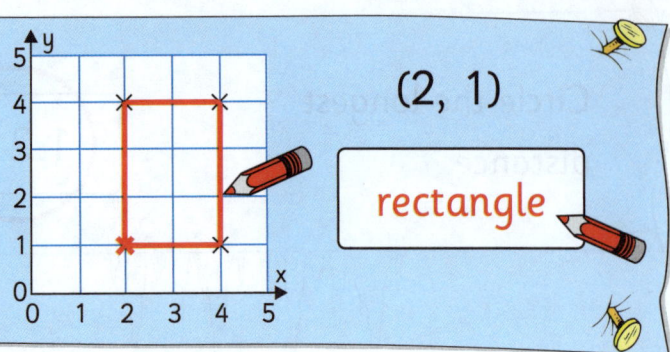
(2, 1) rectangle

1. 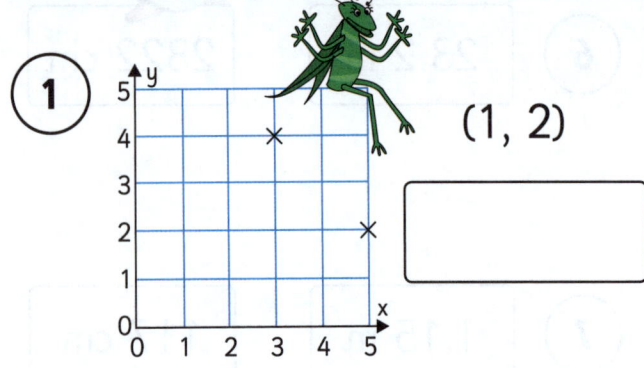 (1, 2)

4. 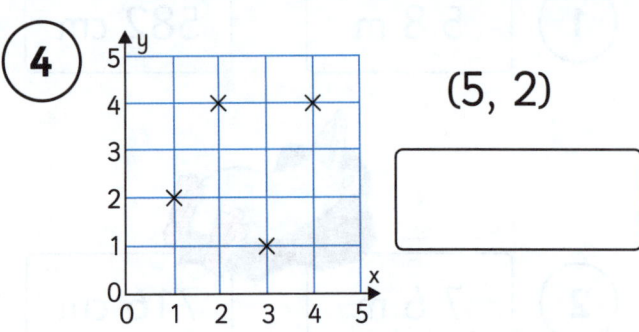 (5, 2)

2. 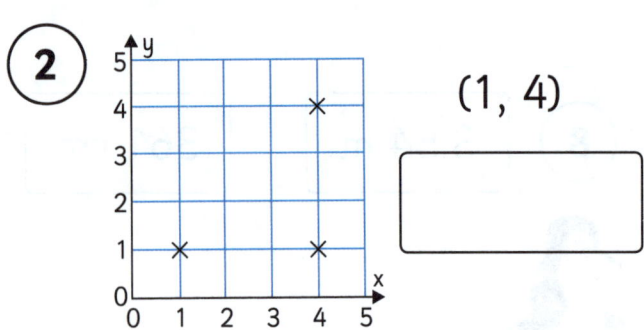 (1, 4)

5. 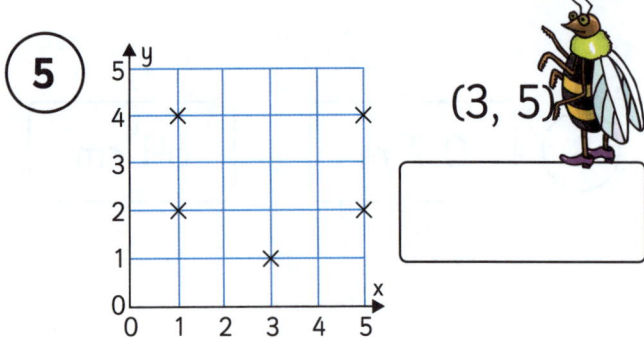 (3, 5)

3. (3, 4)

6. (0, 2)

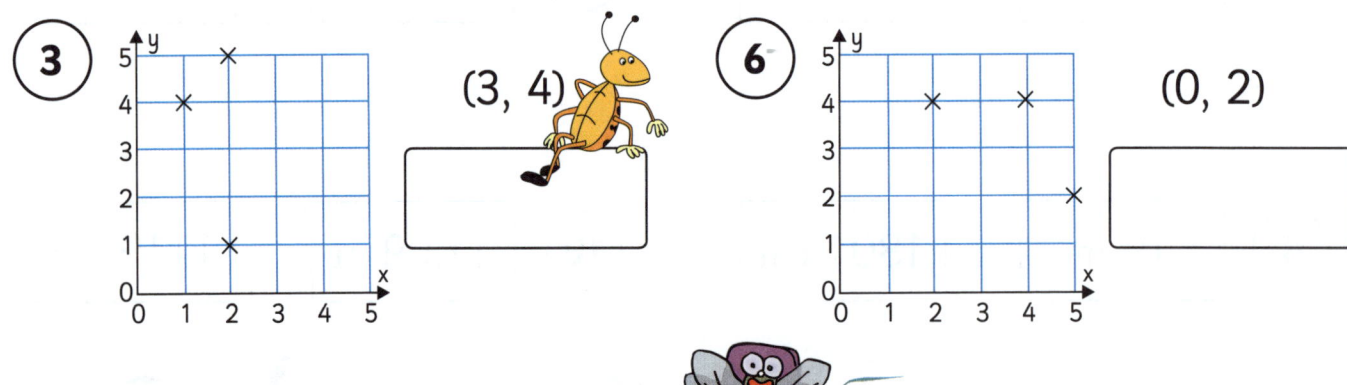

Today I scored ☐ out of 6.

Year 5 Maths — Autumn Term

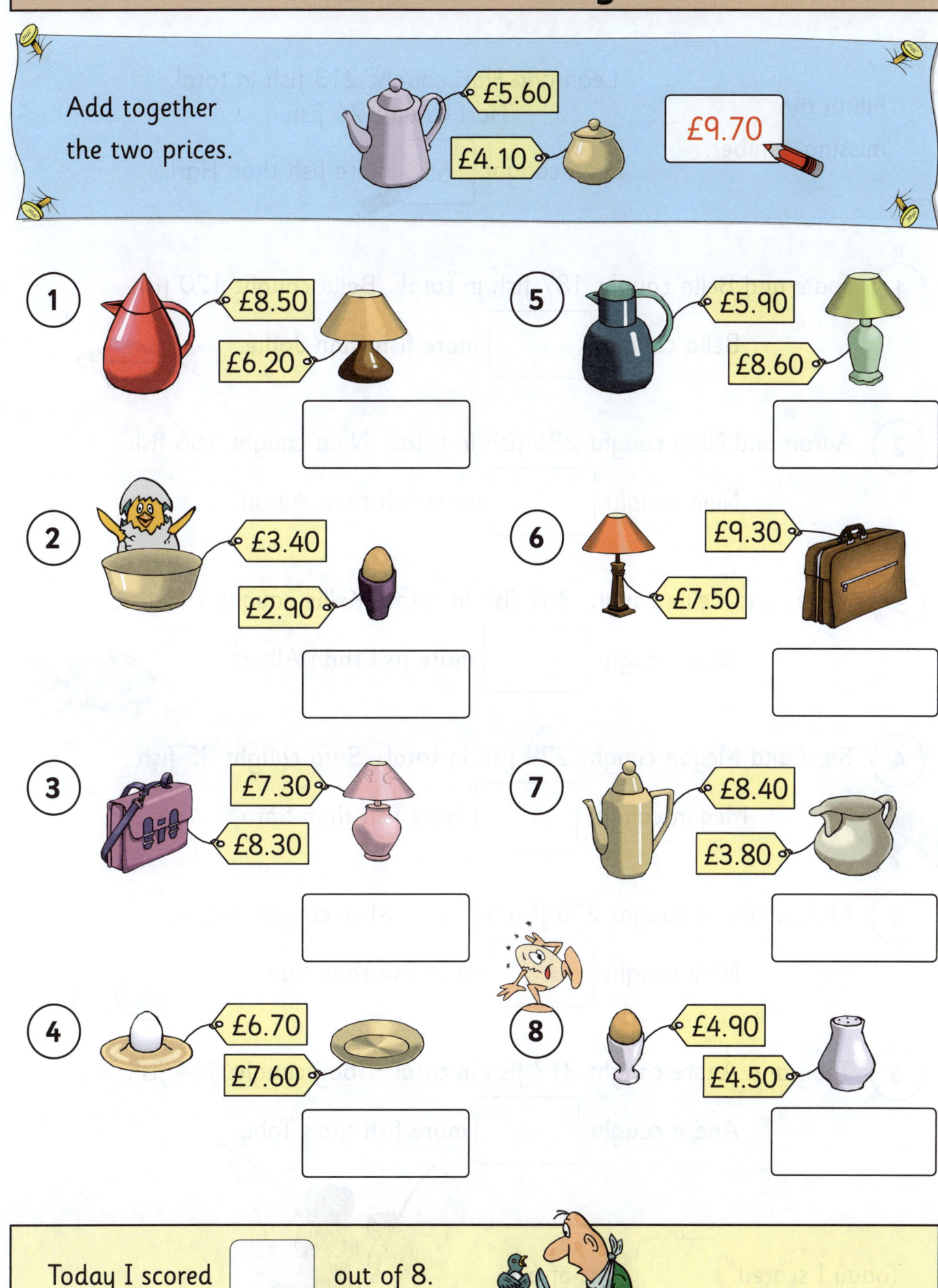

# Week 2 — Day 1

**Fill in the missing number.**

Leah and Hari caught 213 fish in total. Hari caught 74 fish.

Leah caught 65 more fish than Hari.

1) Jodie and Bella caught 187 fish in total. Bella caught 120 fish.

   Bella caught ☐ more fish than Jodie.

2) Aaron and Nina caught 236 fish in total. Nina caught 166 fish.

   Nina caught ☐ more fish than Aaron.

3) Albert and Kellie caught 302 fish in total. Kellie caught 193 fish.

   Kellie caught ☐ more fish than Albert.

4) Sara and Megan caught 229 fish in total. Sara caught 95 fish.

   Megan caught ☐ more fish than Sara.

5) Mick and Liza caught 215 fish in total. Mick caught 138 fish.

   Mick caught ☐ more fish than Liza.

6) Toby and Andre caught 317 fish in total. Toby caught 154 fish.

   Andre caught ☐ more fish than Toby.

Today I scored ☐ out of 6.

# Week 2 — Day 2

Work out the answer to the multiplication.

$$283 \times 6 = 1698$$

```
  283
×   6
-----
 1698
  4 1
```

1) 171 × 8 =

2) 506 × 7 =

3) 394 × 4 =

4) 579 × 3 =

5) 814 × 6 =

6) 492 × 9 =

7) 428 × 3 =

8) 657 × 6 =

9) 517 × 5 =

10) 675 × 9 =

Today I scored ☐ out of 10.

# Week 2 — Day 3

Work out the answer to the division.

360 ÷ 6 = 60

1) 400 ÷ 8 =

2) 330 ÷ 3 =

3) 150 ÷ 5 =

4) 824 ÷ 2 =

5) 540 ÷ 9 =

6) 720 ÷ 8 =

7) 440 ÷ 4 =

8) 320 ÷ 8 =

9) 606 ÷ 6 =

10) 630 ÷ 9 =

11) 240 ÷ 8 =

12) 450 ÷ 5 =

Today I scored ☐ out of 12.

# Week 2 — Day 4

The graph shows how far a boat travelled in the first 12 minutes of a journey. Fill in the missing number.

The boat had travelled **15** miles after 9 minutes.

**1** The boat had travelled ☐ miles after 10 minutes.

**2** The boat had travelled ☐ miles after 4 minutes.

**3** The boat had travelled ☐ miles after 6 minutes.

**4** The boat had travelled ☐ miles after 7 minutes.

**5** The boat had travelled ☐ miles after 5 minutes.

**6** The boat had travelled ☐ miles after 9 minutes.

Today I scored ☐ out of 6.

# Week 2 — Day 5

Fill in the missing number.  $\dfrac{1}{6} = \dfrac{2}{12}$

1) $\dfrac{1}{2} = \dfrac{\boxed{\phantom{0}}}{6}$

2) $\dfrac{1}{5} = \dfrac{\boxed{\phantom{0}}}{10}$

3) $\dfrac{1}{3} = \dfrac{\boxed{\phantom{0}}}{9}$

4) $\dfrac{1}{4} = \dfrac{\boxed{\phantom{0}}}{16}$

5) $\dfrac{1}{7} = \dfrac{\boxed{\phantom{0}}}{21}$

6) $\dfrac{1}{10} = \dfrac{\boxed{\phantom{0}}}{50}$

7) $\dfrac{1}{6} = \dfrac{\boxed{\phantom{0}}}{24}$

8) $\dfrac{1}{9} = \dfrac{\boxed{\phantom{0}}}{36}$

9) $\dfrac{1}{3} = \dfrac{\boxed{\phantom{0}}}{27}$

10) $\dfrac{1}{4} = \dfrac{\boxed{\phantom{0}}}{44}$

11) $\dfrac{1}{7} = \dfrac{\boxed{\phantom{0}}}{56}$

12) $\dfrac{1}{8} = \dfrac{\boxed{\phantom{0}}}{96}$

Today I scored ☐ out of 12.

Year 5 Maths — Autumn Term

# Week 3 — Day 1

Fill in the missing numbers in the sequence.   6, 18, **30**, **42**, **54**, **66**

1) 4, 10, ☐, ☐, ☐, ☐

2) 109, 129, ☐, ☐, ☐, ☐

3) 56, 49, ☐, ☐, ☐, ☐

4) 4321, 5321, ☐, ☐, ☐, ☐

5) 42, 51, ☐, ☐, ☐, ☐

6) 1223, 1373, ☐, ☐, ☐, ☐

7) 682, 657, ☐, ☐, ☐, ☐

8) 410, 485, ☐, ☐, ☐, ☐

Today I scored ☐ out of 8.

# Week 3 — Day 2

The diagram shows the tiles on a patio. Calculate the perimeter of the patio.

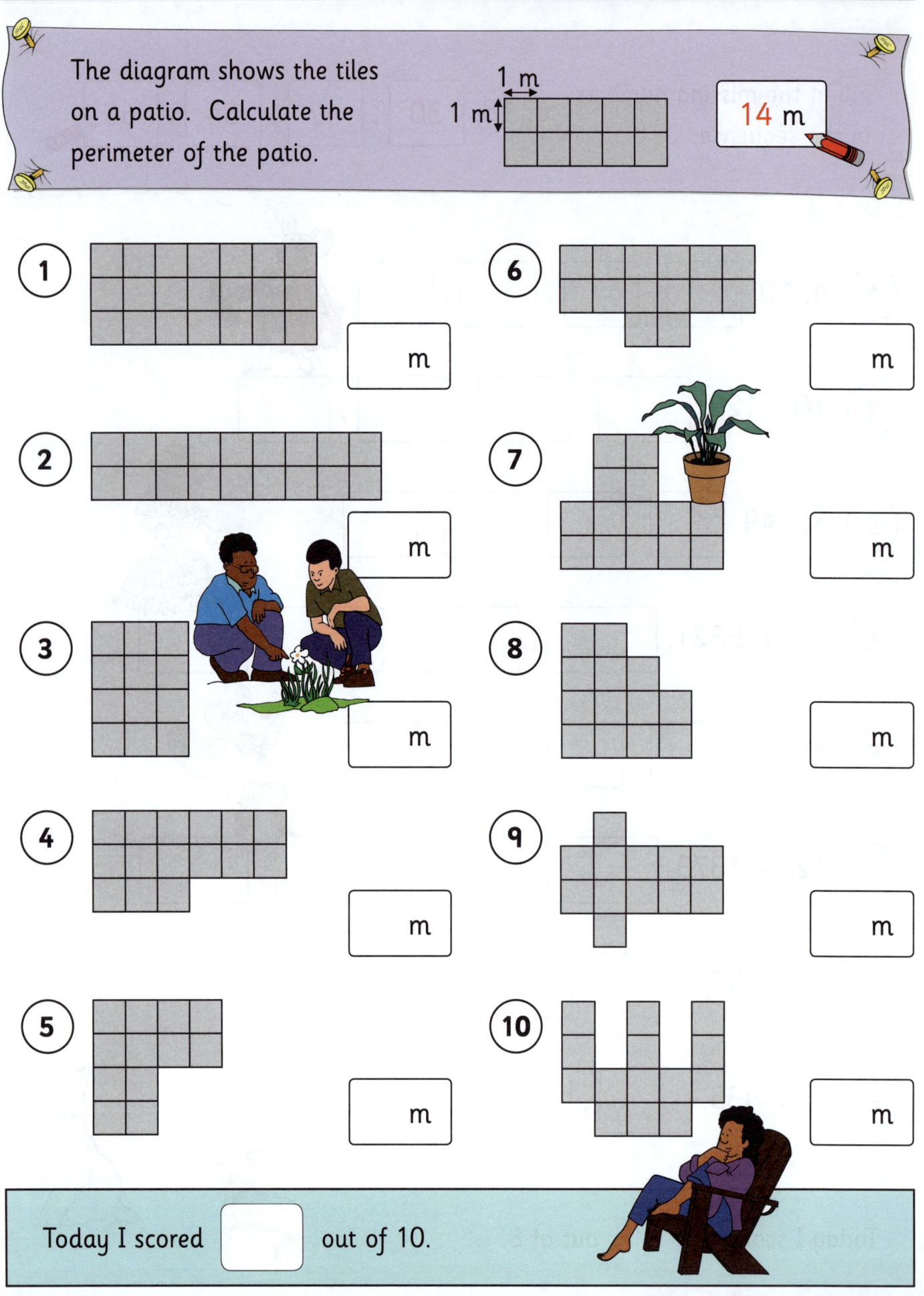

Today I scored ☐ out of 10.

# Week 3 — Day 3

Circle the calculation that is the best estimate for the sum.

14.2 + 8.8 →
- 14 + 8
- 13 + 9
- (14 + 9)

1) 7.1 + 5.9 →
- 7 + 5
- 7 + 6
- 8 + 6

2) 12.8 + 3.3 →
- 13 + 3
- 12 + 3
- 13 + 4

3) 4.2 + 17.2 →
- 4 + 16
- 4 + 17
- 5 + 17

4) 2.9 + 8.7 →
- 2 + 8
- 3 + 9
- 3 + 8

5) 21.7 + 19.1 →
- 22 + 20
- 21 + 19
- 22 + 19

6) 20.9 + 1.2 →
- 20 + 1
- 21 + 1
- 21 + 2

7) 10.9 + 6.2 →
- 10 + 6
- 11 + 7
- 11 + 6

8) 11.2 + 0.8 →
- 11 + 1
- 11 + 0
- 12 + 1

9) 9.7 + 9.3 →
- 9 + 9
- 10 + 9
- 10 + 10

10) 4.6 + 6.4 →
- 5 + 6
- 4 + 6
- 5 + 7

Today I scored ☐ out of 10.

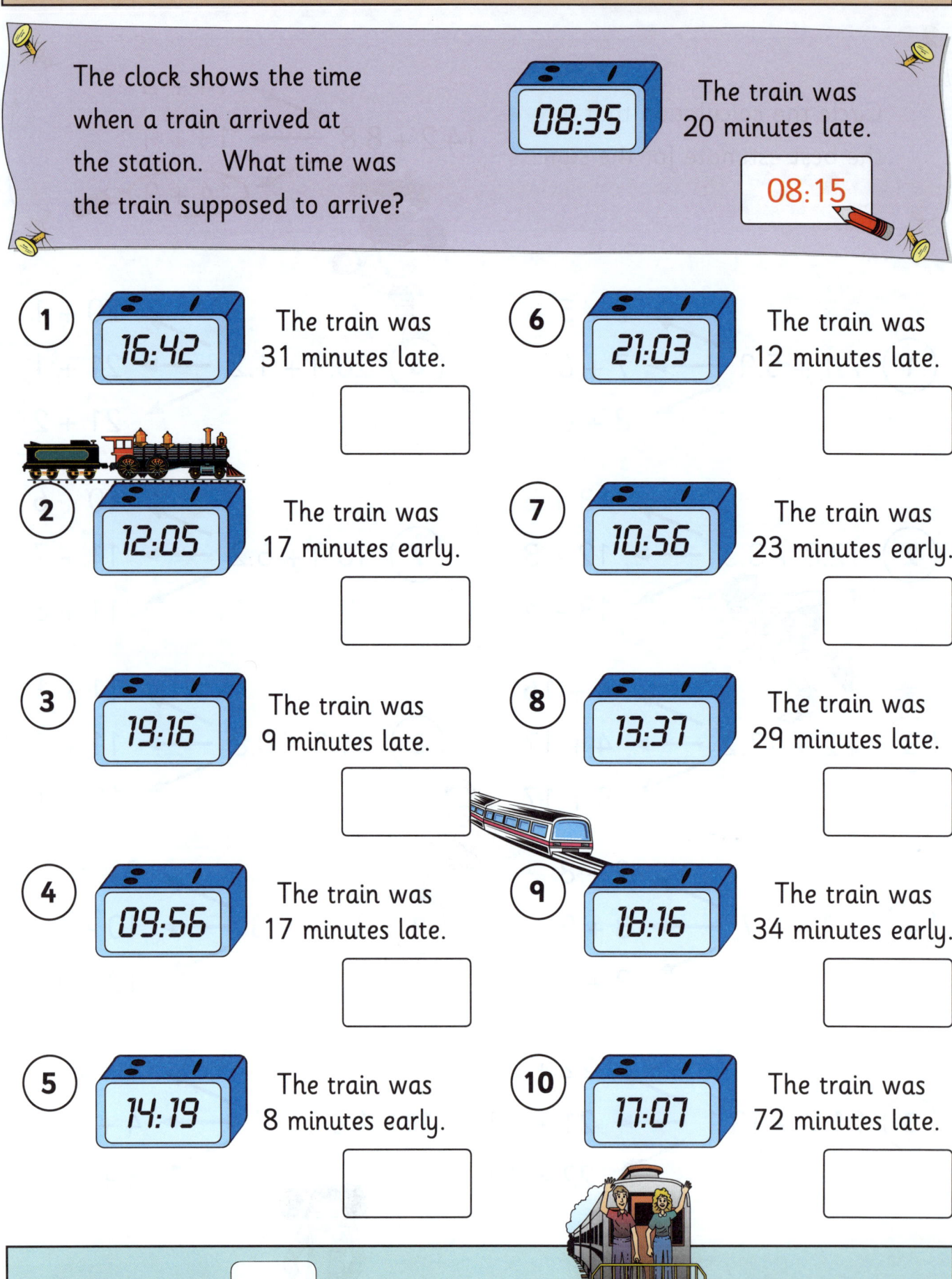

# Week 3 — Day 5

Work out the distance between the two steps.

The distance between the steps on a ladder is 40 cm. What is the distance between the 4th and the 6th step?

80 cm

1. The distance between the steps on a ladder is 25 cm. What is the distance between the 2nd and the 5th step? ___ cm

2. The distance between the steps on a ladder is 30 cm. What is the distance between the 4th and the 8th step? ___ cm

3. The distance between the steps on a ladder is 40 cm. What is the distance between the 3rd and the 9th step? ___ cm

4. The distance between the steps on a ladder is 20 cm. What is the distance between the 5th and the 7th step? ___ cm

5. The distance between the steps on a ladder is 30 cm. What is the distance between the 2nd and the 10th step? ___ cm

6. The distance between the steps on a ladder is 40 cm. What is the distance between the 1st and the 5th step? ___ cm

7. The distance between the steps on a ladder is 25 cm. What is the distance between the 3rd and the 10th step? ___ cm

8. The distance between the steps on a ladder is 30 cm. What is the distance between the 4th and the 9th step? ___ cm

Today I scored ___ out of 8.

# Week 4 — Day 1

Write the number using digits.   Four hundred and fifty thousand, one hundred and twelve   450 112

1) Eighty one thousand, six hundred and four

2) One hundred and two thousand, three hundred and forty one

3) Seven hundred and twenty thousand, four hundred and sixty six

4) Three hundred and fifty four thousand and seventy one

5) Thirty thousand and sixteen

6) Two hundred and eleven thousand, five hundred and nine

7) Nine hundred and five thousand, six hundred and thirteen

8) Six hundred and ninety thousand, eight hundred and fifty

Today I scored ☐ out of 8.

# Week 4 — Day 2

**Complete the sequence by filling in the next four numbers.**

**Count up in steps of 100:**

5765, **5865**, **5965**, **6065**, **6165**

**1)** Count up in steps of 1000:

10 502, ____, ____, ____, ____

**2)** Count backwards in steps of 100:

42 357, ____, ____, ____, ____

**3)** Count up in steps of 10 000:

281 650, ____, ____, ____, ____

**4)** Count up in steps of 100:

50 710, ____, ____, ____, ____

**5)** Count backwards in steps of 100 000:

491 081, ____, ____, ____, ____

**6)** Count backwards in steps of 10 000:

40 023, ____, ____, ____, ____

Today I scored ____ out of 6.

# Week 4 — Day 3

Put these numbers in order from smallest to largest.   49 201, 48 853, 49 075, 48 899

| 48 853 | 48 899 | 49 075 | 49 201 |

**1)** 5836, 6123, 6098, 5774

**2)** 110 622, 98 407, 94 951, 108 328

**3)** 37 615, 37 053, 37 590, 37 712

**4)** 205 674, 205 720, 204 836, 204 691

**5)** 572 862, 570 650, 572 872, 570 885

**6)** 433 919, 434 008, 433 892, 433 913

Today I scored ☐ out of 6.

# Week 4 — Day 4

Shade in one square so that the dotted line is a line of symmetry.

1.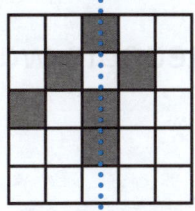
2.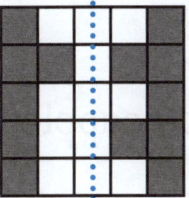
3.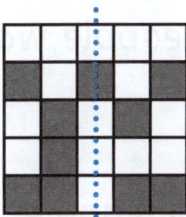
4.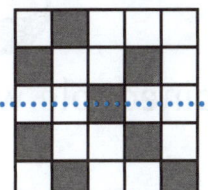
5.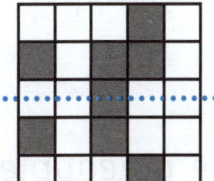

6.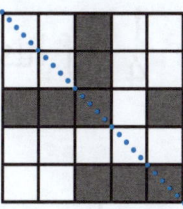
7.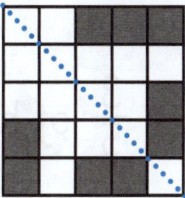
8.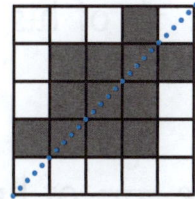
9.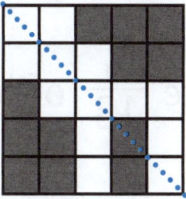
10.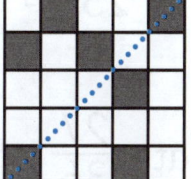

Today I scored ☐ out of 10.

# Week 4 — Day 5

Alice and her friends had one pineapple each. Work out the fraction of the pineapple that is left.

Alice ate $\frac{2}{3}$ of her pineapple.

$\frac{1}{3}$ of the pineapple was left.

1) Basri ate $\frac{1}{4}$ of his pineapple. ☐ of the pineapple was left.

2) Chiara ate $\frac{5}{6}$ of her pineapple. ☐ of the pineapple was left.

3) Dahlia ate $\frac{3}{5}$ of her pineapple. ☐ of the pineapple was left.

4) Elliot ate $\frac{4}{9}$ of his pineapple. ☐ of the pineapple was left.

5) Fiona ate $\frac{9}{14}$ of her pineapple. ☐ of the pineapple was left.

6) Grant ate $\frac{5}{13}$ of his pineapple. ☐ of the pineapple was left.

7) Hasan ate $\frac{9}{25}$ of his pineapple. ☐ of the pineapple was left.

8) Imogen ate $\frac{27}{36}$ of her pineapple. ☐ of the pineapple was left.

Today I scored ☐ out of 8.

# Week 5 — Day 1

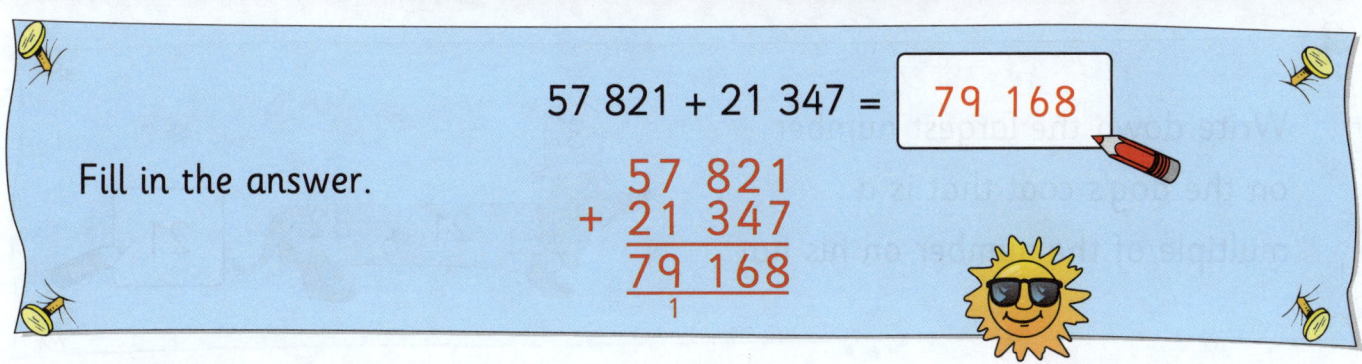

57 821 + 21 347 = 79 168

```
  57 821
+ 21 347
  79 168
       1
```

Fill in the answer.

1) 14 733 + 32 092 =

2) 23 628 + 41 572 =

3) 69 232 + 5826 =

4) 78 665 + 9873 =

5) 3.56 + 4.28 =

6) 72.53 + 8.26 =

7) 2.81 + 1.7 =

8) 31.9 + 5.68 =

Today I scored ☐ out of 8.

# Week 5 — Day 2

Write down the largest number on the dog's coat that is a multiple of the number on his hat.

Example: hat 3, coat 1, 21, 6, 32 → **21**

1. Hat: 2; Coat: 22, 21, 8, 36
2. Hat: 5; Coat: 26, 76, 65, 15
3. Hat: 10; Coat: 75, 70, 15, 20
4. Hat: 4; Coat: 2, 24, 12, 54
5. Hat: 9; Coat: 81, 89, 27, 36
6. Hat: 6; Coat: 66, 74, 76, 72
7. Hat: 7; Coat: 14, 49, 35, 29
8. Hat: 8; Coat: 88, 96, 84, 98
9. Hat: 11; Coat: 66, 39, 78, 22
10. Hat: 12; Coat: 96, 48, 54, 98
11. Hat: 20; Coat: 90, 50, 40, 80
12. Hat: 15; Coat: 30, 75, 35, 80

Today I scored ☐ out of 12.

Year 5 Maths — Autumn Term

# Week 5 — Day 3

Write down all the factor pairs for each number. Circle the common factors.

15 → ①× 15, 3 ×⑤

20 → ①× 20, 2 × 10, 4 ×⑤

**1)** 9 →

12 →

**2)** 6 →

18 →

**3)** 5 →

30 →

**4)** 10 →

45 →

**5)** 4 →

24 →

**6)** 21 →

36 →

Today I scored ☐ out of 6.

# Week 5 — Day 4

Change the time taken into the units shown.

2 hours → **120** minutes

1) 4 hours → ☐ minutes

2) 5 minutes → ☐ seconds

3) 2 days → ☐ hours

4) 3 years → ☐ months

5) 8 weeks → ☐ days

6) 1 hour 15 minutes → ☐ minutes

7) 3 minutes 30 seconds → ☐ seconds

8) 10 days 4 hours → ☐ hours

9) 2 years 5 months → ☐ months

10) 6 weeks 3 days → ☐ days

Today I scored ☐ out of 10.

# Week 5 — Day 5

Circle the two fractions that are equivalent in each set.

$\boxed{\enclose{circle}{\dfrac{2}{3}} \quad \enclose{circle}{\dfrac{6}{9}} \quad \dfrac{3}{4}}$

1) $\dfrac{4}{10}$    $\dfrac{1}{4}$    $\dfrac{2}{5}$

2) $\dfrac{3}{4}$    $\dfrac{8}{10}$    $\dfrac{75}{100}$

3) $\dfrac{1}{2}$    $\dfrac{1}{3}$    $\dfrac{2}{6}$

4) $\dfrac{5}{20}$    $\dfrac{1}{4}$    $\dfrac{2}{5}$

5) $\dfrac{6}{10}$    $\dfrac{1}{3}$    $\dfrac{3}{5}$

6) $\dfrac{10}{20}$    $\dfrac{1}{2}$    $\dfrac{6}{10}$

7) $\dfrac{3}{12}$    $\dfrac{1}{3}$    $\dfrac{1}{4}$

8) $\dfrac{77}{100}$    $\dfrac{14}{20}$    $\dfrac{7}{10}$

9) $\dfrac{5}{6}$    $\dfrac{15}{20}$    $\dfrac{10}{12}$

10) $\dfrac{16}{20}$    $\dfrac{4}{5}$    $\dfrac{6}{10}$

11) $\dfrac{10}{25}$    $\dfrac{5}{15}$    $\dfrac{1}{3}$

12) $\dfrac{2}{20}$    $\dfrac{40}{100}$    $\dfrac{2}{5}$

Today I scored ☐ out of 12.

# Week 6 — Day 1

Look at the grid. Write down the coordinates of points A and B.

A (3, 2)
B (4, 5)

1. A ____  B ____

2. A ____  B ____

3. A ____  B ____

4. A ____  B ____

5. A ____  B ____

6. A ____  B ____

Today I scored ____ out of 6.

# Week 6 — Day 2

Work out the answer to the subtraction.

34 889 − 22 593 = 12 296

```
   7 1
 3 4 8̷ 8̷ 9
−2 2 5 9 3
 1 2 2 9 6
```

1) 6849 − 2315 =

2) 7932 − 6401 =

3) 82 764 − 1652 =

4) 43 678 − 3465 =

5) 87 294 − 64 168 =

6) 49 337 − 24 419 =

7) 36 210 − 3148 =

8) 27 026 − 8519 =

Today I scored ☐ out of 8.

# Week 6 — Day 3

Circle the most sensible answer.

Innes is  0.12 m   12 m   **(1.2 m)**  tall.

1) Kamil's feet are  2 cm   200 cm   20 cm  long.

2) Mikaela weighs  45 kg   450 kg   0.45 kg .

3) Themba's house is  12.5 m   1250 m   1.25 m  tall.

4) Ajay's pet earthworm is  630 mm   63 mm   6.3 mm  long.

5) Philip's pet mouse weighs  20 g   200 g   2 g .

6) Poppy drives  7.5 km   0.075 km   750 km  to get to work.

7) Chloe's glass holds  2.5 ml   2500 ml   250 ml  of lemonade.

8) Rani uses  1 l   100 l   1000 l  of water for his bath.

Today I scored [ ] out of 8.

# Week 6 — Day 4

Work out the answer to the subtraction.

$35.7 - 3.8 = \boxed{31.9}$

$$\begin{array}{r} 3\overset{4}{\cancel{5}}.\overset{1}{7} \\ -\phantom{0}3.8 \\ \hline 31.9 \end{array}$$

1) $78.9 - 36.2 = \boxed{\phantom{00}}$

2) $58.2 - 27.3 = \boxed{\phantom{00}}$

3) $31.78 - 22.69 = \boxed{\phantom{00}}$

4) $59.32 - 6.44 = \boxed{\phantom{00}}$

5) $61.51 - 31.2 = \boxed{\phantom{00}}$

6) $87.01 - 2.32 = \boxed{\phantom{00}}$

7) $38.67 - 15.3 = \boxed{\phantom{00}}$

8) $47.64 - 3.7 = \boxed{\phantom{00}}$

Today I scored ☐ out of 8.

# Week 6 — Day 5

Use rounding to check if the answer to the calculation is sensible. Put a tick if the answer is reasonable and a cross if it isn't.

5236 + 4967 = 10 203

5000 + 5000 = 10 000 ✓

1) 238 + 695 = 933

2) 479 − 312 = 57

3) 5962 + 8211 = 9137

4) 9098 − 837 = 8261

5) 3.7 + 2.1 = 5.8

6) 14.3 − 5.8 = 8.5

7) 7.91 + 6.23 = 23.64

8) 39.6 − 27.5 = 12.1

9) 54.8 + 70.4 = 80.2

10) 102.9 + 67.05 = 169.95

11) 17.63 − 12.69 = 4.94

12) 108.09 − 9.55 = 53.04

Today I scored [ ] out of 12.

# Week 7 — Day 1

Fill in the missing number.  50 000 − 2100 = 47 900

1) 15 000 + ☐ = 18 500

2) 7600 − 800 = ☐

3) 40 100 + 3300 = ☐

4) ☐ − 32 000 = 19 600

5) 700 + ☐ = 35 100

6) ☐ − 10 400 = 29 900

7) 25 300 − ☐ = 9200

8) 4500 + ☐ = 60 500

9) 18 700 − 9200 = ☐

10) ☐ + 14 600 = 30 000

11) ☐ = 97 000 − 2800

12) 62 900 − 6300 = ☐

Today I scored ☐ out of 12.

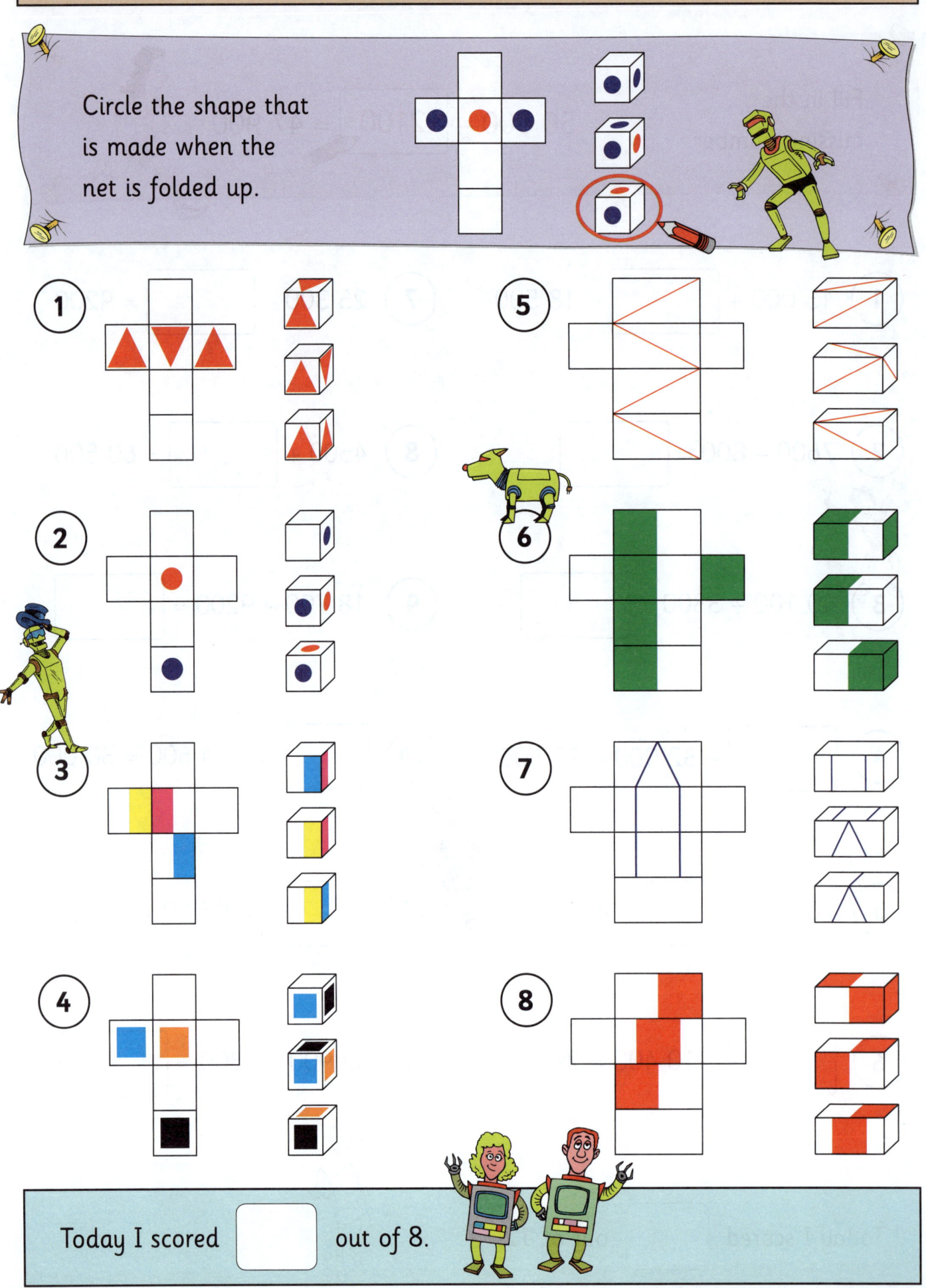

# Week 7 — Day 3

Deepa has £9.60. She buys some cakes and has some money left over. Work out the missing price.

£1.20 left over    £7.90

**1**

£5.11 left over

**5**

£4.12 left over

**2**

£1.90 left over

**6**

£7.10 left over

**3**

£8.20 left over

**7**

£5.40 left over

**4**

£2.36 left over

**8**

£5.13 left over

Today I scored ☐ out of 8.

# Week 7 — Day 4

Fill in the missing number.    $4 \times 6 = 3 \times \boxed{8}$

1) $2 \times 8 = 4 \times \boxed{\phantom{0}}$

2) $5 \times 4 = \boxed{\phantom{0}} \times 10$

3) $5 \times \boxed{\phantom{0}} = 6 \times 10$

4) $2 \times 15 = 6 \times \boxed{\phantom{0}}$

5) $2 \times 9 = \boxed{\phantom{0}} \times 3$

6) $6 \times 7 = 14 \times \boxed{\phantom{0}}$

7) $\boxed{\phantom{0}} \times 10 = 8 \times 5$

8) $5 \times \boxed{\phantom{0}} = 2 \times 20$

9) $4 \times 8 = 2 \times \boxed{\phantom{0}}$

10) $6 \times \boxed{\phantom{0}} = 3 \times 16$

11) $6 \times 10 = 4 \times \boxed{\phantom{0}}$

12) $3 \times \boxed{\phantom{0}} = 4 \times 9$

Today I scored $\boxed{\phantom{0}}$ out of 12.

# Week 7 — Day 5

Complete the pictogram showing the colours of cars in a car park.

Key: 🔵 = 4 cars

| Colour | Number of cars | Total |
|---|---|---|
| White | 🔵🔵🔵 | 12 |
| Silver | 🔵🔵🔵🔵◗ | 18 |
| Orange | 🔴🔴 | 8 |

**1** Key: 🔵 = 5 cars

| Colour | Number of cars | Total |
|---|---|---|
| Blue | 🔵🔵 | |
| Black | 🔵🔵🔵 | |
| Purple | 🔵🔵🔵🔵🔵 | |

**2** Key: 🔵 = 2 cars

| Colour | Number of cars | Total |
|---|---|---|
| Gold | 🔵🔵🔵🔵◗ | |
| Silver | | 3 |
| Bronze | | 8 |

**3** Key: 🔵 = 3 cars

| Colour | Number of cars | Total |
|---|---|---|
| Red | | 9 |
| Green | | 6 |
| Pink | 🔵🔵🔵🔵 | |

**4** Key: 🔵 = 10 cars

| Colour | Number of cars | Total |
|---|---|---|
| Grey | | 10 |
| Beige | 🔵🔵🔵◗ | |
| Cream | | 45 |

**5** Key: 🔵 = 8 cars

| Colour | Number of cars | Total |
|---|---|---|
| Brown | | 40 |
| Yellow | 🔵🔵🔵◗ | |
| Green | | 12 |

**6** Key: 🔵 = ☐ cars

| Colour | Number of cars | Total |
|---|---|---|
| Blue | 🔵🔵🔵🔵🔵 | 20 |
| Pink | 🔵🔵🔵◗ | |
| Black | | 16 |

Today I scored ☐ out of 6.

# Week 8 — Day 1

Write the decimal as a fraction of 100.   0.5 as a fraction of 100 is $\frac{50}{100}$

1. 0.17 as a fraction of 100 is
2. 0.66 as a fraction of 100 is
3. 0.09 as a fraction of 100 is
4. 0.25 as a fraction of 100 is
5. 0.44 as a fraction of 100 is
6. 0.36 as a fraction of 100 is
7. 0.01 as a fraction of 100 is
8. 0.1 as a fraction of 100 is
9. 0.08 as a fraction of 100 is
10. 0.99 as a fraction of 100 is
11. 0.4 as a fraction of 100 is
12. 0.7 as a fraction of 100 is

Today I scored ___ out of 12.

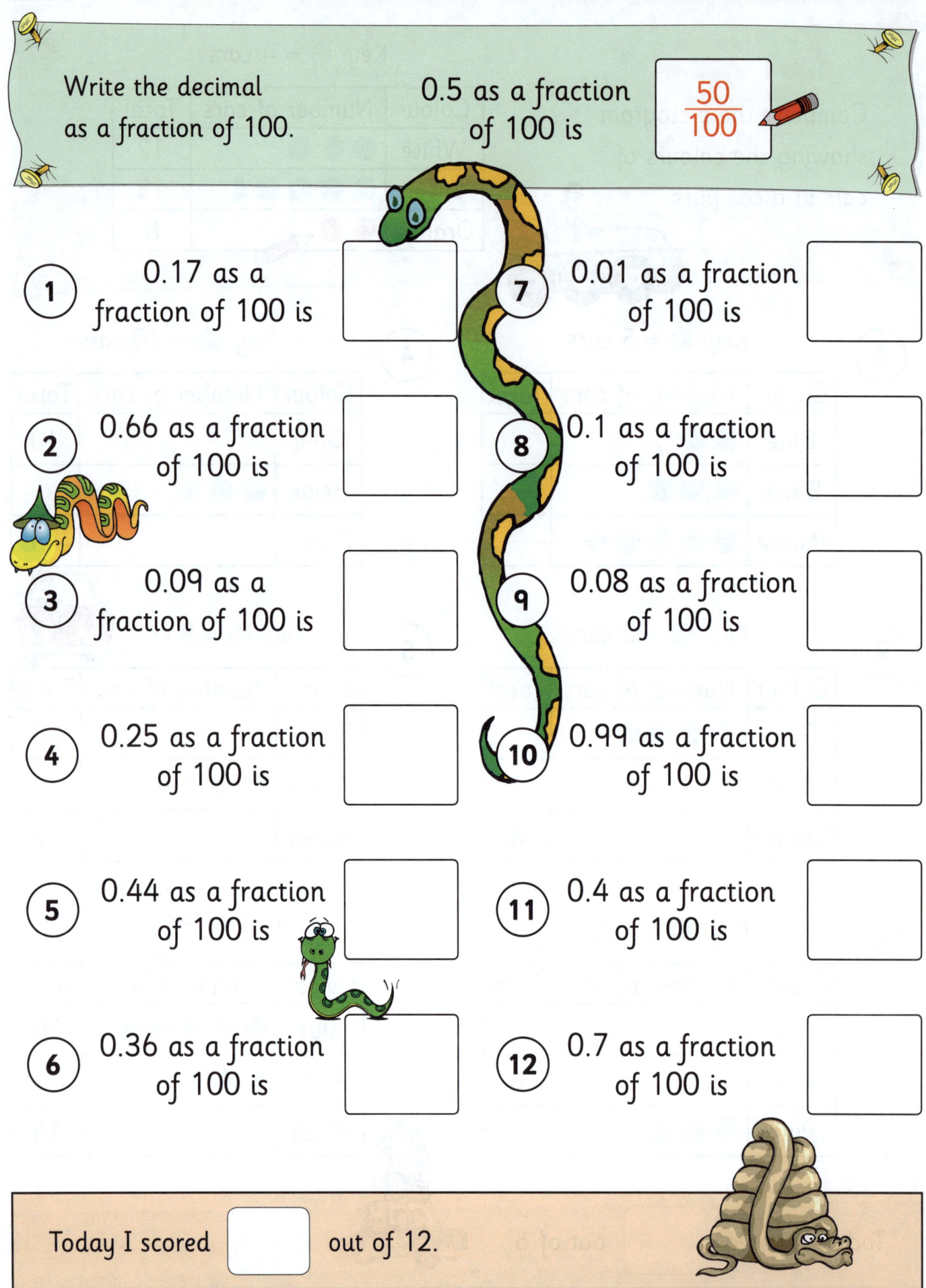

# Week 8 — Day 2

Fill in the answer.   23 × 10 = 230

1) 7 × 10 =

2) 120 ÷ 10 =

3) 456 × 10 =

4) 900 ÷ 100 =

5) 55 × 1000 =

6) 371 ÷ 10 =

7) 4.38 × 10 =

8) 220 ÷ 1000 =

9) 8.91 × 100 =

10) 778.5 ÷ 10 =

11) 3.46 × 1000 =

12) 33.4 ÷ 100 =

Today I scored ☐ out of 12.

# Week 8 — Day 3

Look at these angles. Circle the angle which matches the description.

**an acute angle**

1. an obtuse angle
2. a right angle
3. an acute angle
4. equal to two right angles
5. bigger than two right angles
6. between one and two right angles
7. half a right angle
8. smaller than three right angles

Today I scored ☐ out of 8.

# Week 8 — Day 4

Leah and Wade are sharing sweets. Leah always gets twice as many sweets as Wade. How many sweets do they each get?

They share 72 sweets.

Leah [ 48 ]   Wade [ 24 ]

1) They share 27 sweets.

   Leah [ ]   Wade [ ]

2) They share 99 sweets.

   Leah [ ]   Wade [ ]

3) They share 51 sweets.

   Leah [ ]   Wade [ ]

4) They share 114 sweets.

   Leah [ ]   Wade [ ]

5) They share 231 sweets.

   Leah [ ]   Wade [ ]

6) They share 324 sweets.

   Leah [ ]   Wade [ ]

7) They share 441 sweets.

   Leah [ ]   Wade [ ]

8) They share 825 sweets.

   Leah [ ]   Wade [ ]

Today I scored [ ] out of 8.

# Week 8 — Day 5

Fill in the gap in the calculation.  100 ÷ [10] = 10

1) 25 × ☐ = 2500

2) 840 ÷ 10 = ☐

3) ☐ × 1000 = 35 000

4) 4000 ÷ ☐ = 4

5) 3735 × 10 = ☐

6) ☐ ÷ 1000 = 1

7) 8.9 × ☐ = 89

8) 73 ÷ 10 = ☐

9) ☐ × 67.5 = 6750

10) 22 ÷ ☐ = 0.22

11) 1000 × 0.4 = ☐

12) ☐ ÷ 100 = 3.3

Today I scored ☐ out of 12.

# Week 9 — Day 1

**Round the number to the nearest figure given.**

Round **14** to the nearest 10: **10**

1) Round **87** to the nearest 10:

2) Round **343** to the nearest 10:

3) Round **3655** to the nearest 10:

4) Round **77** to the nearest 100:

5) Round **580** to the nearest 100:

6) Round **1049** to the nearest 100:

7) Round **7300** to the nearest 1000:

8) Round **999 999** to the nearest 100 000:

9) Round **65 010** to the nearest 1000:

10) Round **54 368** to the nearest 10 000:

11) Round **95 300** to the nearest 100 000:

12) Round **324 764** to the nearest 10 000:

Today I scored ☐ out of 12.

# Week 9 — Day 2

Fill in the answer to the calculation.

2721 × 3 = 8163

```
  2721
×    3
  8163
     ²
```

1) 3600 × 6 = ☐

2) 4910 × 4 = ☐

3) 3805 × 7 = ☐

4) 9512 × 8 = ☐

5) 7315 × 2 = ☐

6) 3982 × 6 = ☐

7) 4034 × 4 = ☐

8) 9991 × 9 = ☐

Today I scored ☐ out of 8.

# Week 9 — Day 3

Angelica goes for 5 runs a week. Circle whether the time for all 5 runs is over or under 1 hour.

12 mins, 18 mins, 4 mins, 9 mins, 16 mins

over | **under** (circled)

1) 22 mins, 7 mins, 5 mins, 13 mins, 19 mins
over | under

2) 12 mins, 18 mins, 4 mins, 9 mins, 16 mins
over | under

3) 2 mins, 30 mins, 7 mins, 13 mins, 6 mins
over | under

4) 9 mins, 16 mins, 22 mins, 14 mins, 1 min
over | under

5) 25 mins, 8 mins, 11 mins, 9 mins, 8 mins
over | under

6) 19 mins, 22 mins, 6 mins, 6 mins, 8 mins
over | under

7) 4 mins, 28 mins, 9 mins, 3 mins, 15 mins
over | under

8) 11 mins, 3 mins, 4 mins, 35 mins, 6 mins
over | under

9) 41 mins, 7 mins, 5 mins, 6 mins, 2 mins
over | under

10) 24 mins, 7 mins, 5 mins, 12 mins, 11 mins
over | under

Today I scored ☐ out of 10.

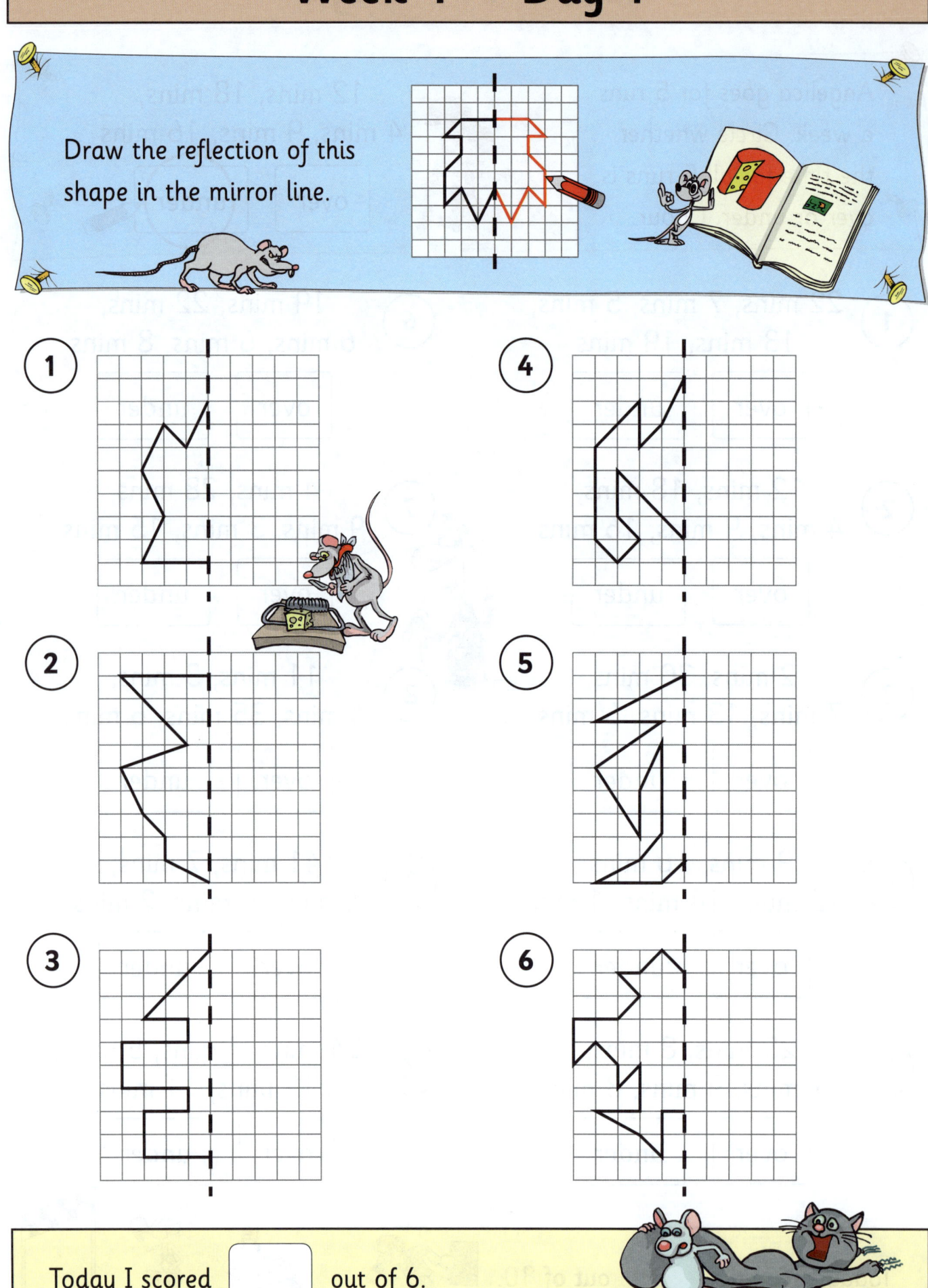

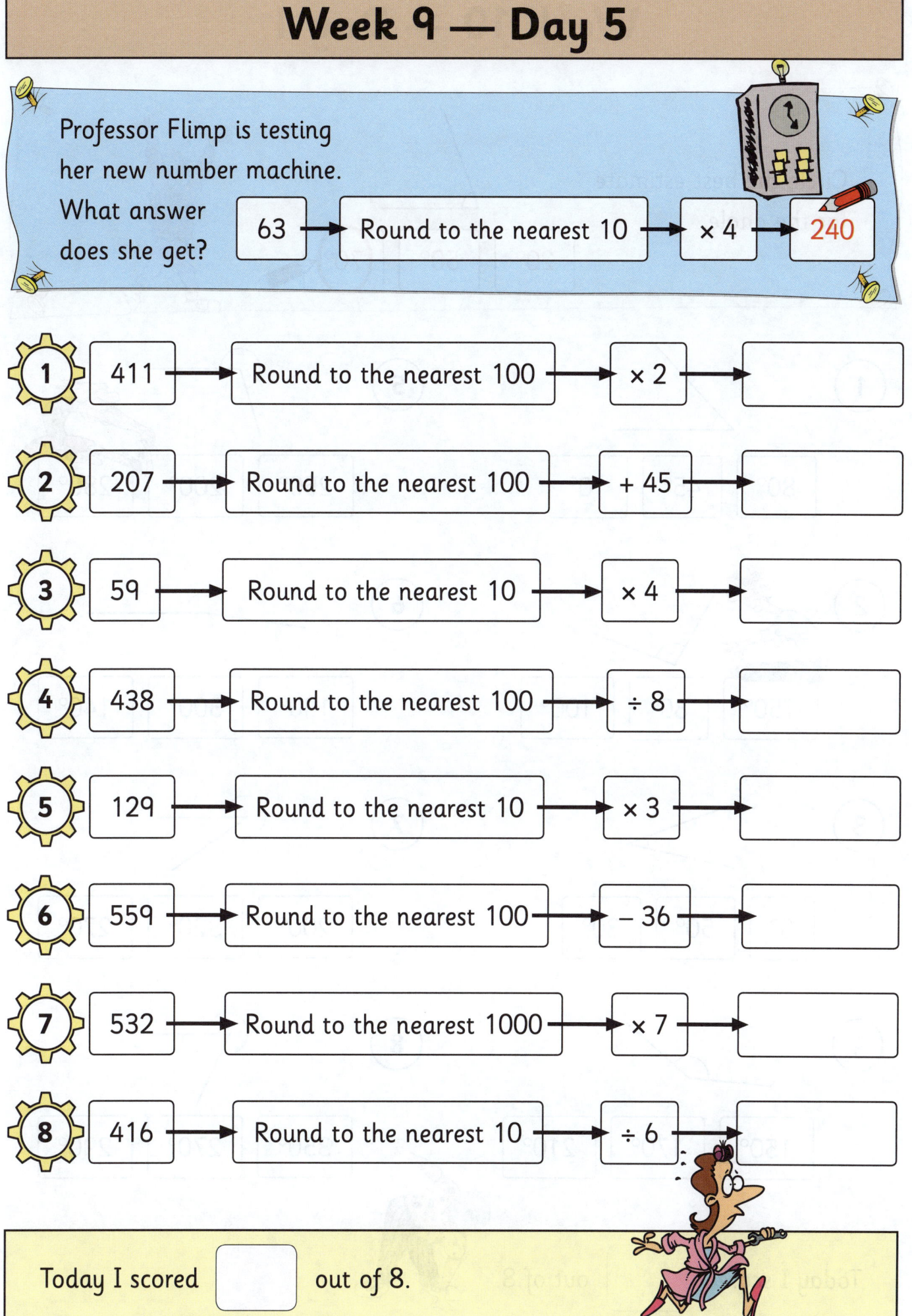

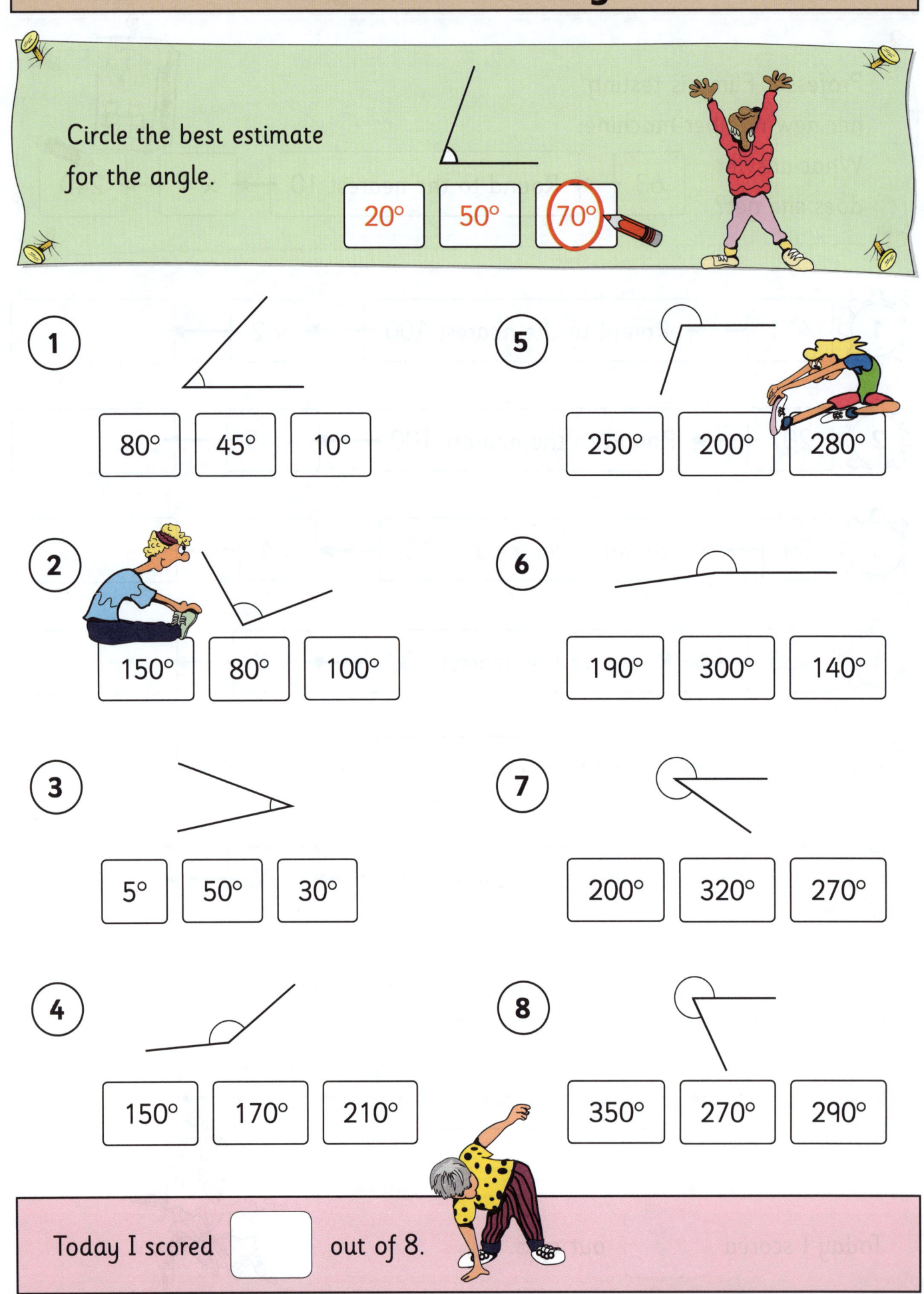

# Week 10 — Day 2

Use the information given to work out the answer to the calculation.

60 × 40 = 2400

61 × 40 = 2440

1) 20 × 35 = 700
   21 × 35 = 

2) 50 × 60 = 3000
   52 × 60 = 

3) 30 × 80 = 2400
   30 × 82 = 

4) 45 × 50 = 2250
   47 × 50 = 

5) 85 × 25 = 2125
   88 × 25 = 

6) 105 × 15 = 1575
   103 × 15 = 

7) 75 × 90 = 6750
   74 × 90 = 

8) 45 × 110 = 4950
   45 × 109 = 

9) 120 × 30 = 3600
   120 × 28 = 

10) 150 × 135 = 20 250
    150 × 134 = 

Today I scored ☐ out of 10.

# Week 10 — Day 3

Match the number to the correct Roman numeral.

10 → X (circled) / V

1. 7 → IIV / VII
2. 14 → XIV / IIX
3. 22 → LXI / XXII
4. 50 → L / XX
5. 100 → LLX / C
6. 56 → XXCI / LVI
7. 33 → XXLVI / XXXIII
8. 67 → XCVII / LXVII
9. 19 → XIX / IXV
10. 49 → XLIX / XXXXIV
11. 84 → XCXXIV / LXXXIV
12. 99 → XCIX / CIXX

Today I scored ☐ out of 12.

# Week 10 — Day 5

Use a protractor to draw the angle.  75°

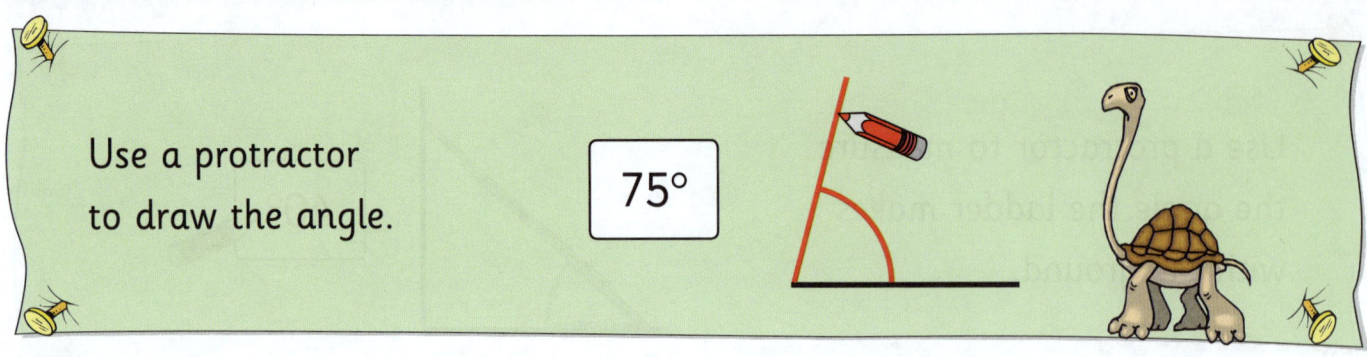

1. 30°

2. 80°

3. 21°

4. 120°

5. 150°

6. 169°

7. 250°

8. 340°

Today I scored ☐ out of 8.

# Week 11 — Day 1

The bar chart shows the number of carrots grown by some farmers. Use the chart to find how many more carrots were grown by the farmer who grew the most carrots than by the farmer who grew the least carrots.

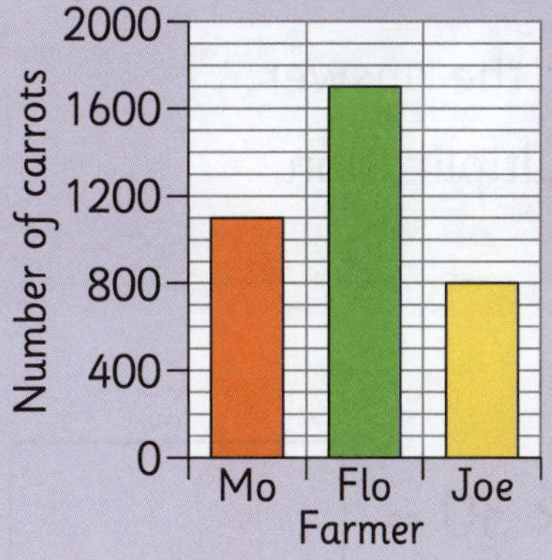

**900**

1) [Al: 1600, Ann: 1200, Ash: 1400]

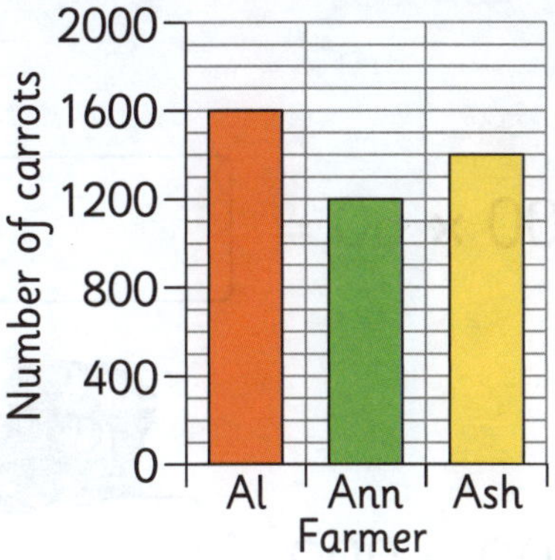

2) [Bea: 1000, Ben: 1100, Brie: 1200]

3) [Cal: 800, Cass: 3600, Chris: 2000]

4) [Dai: 350, Dave: 850, Dot: 800]

5) [Edith: 700, Evan: 150, Eric: 600]

6) [Fae: 4750, Fred: 1250, Finn: 1500]

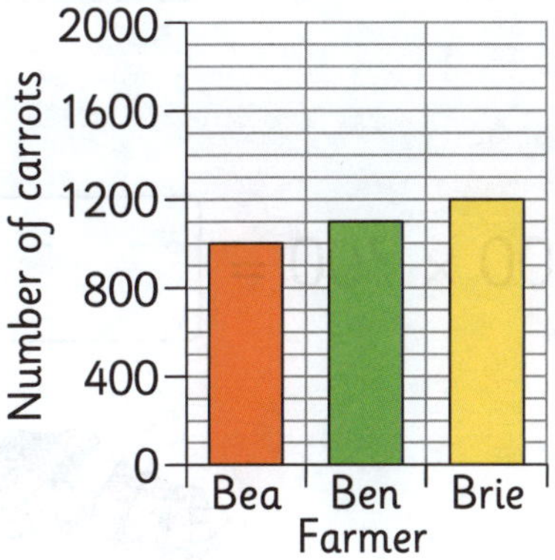

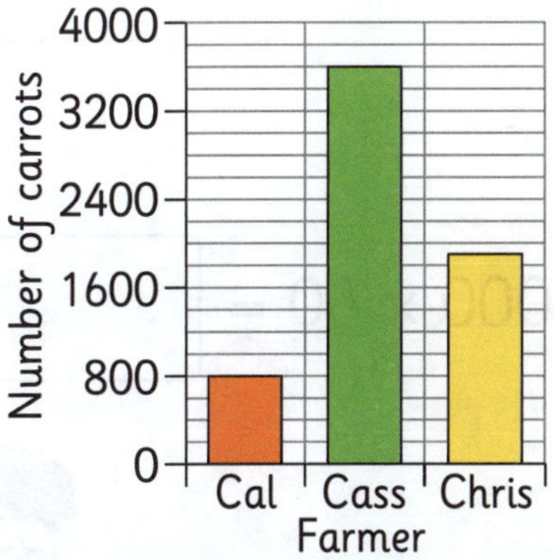

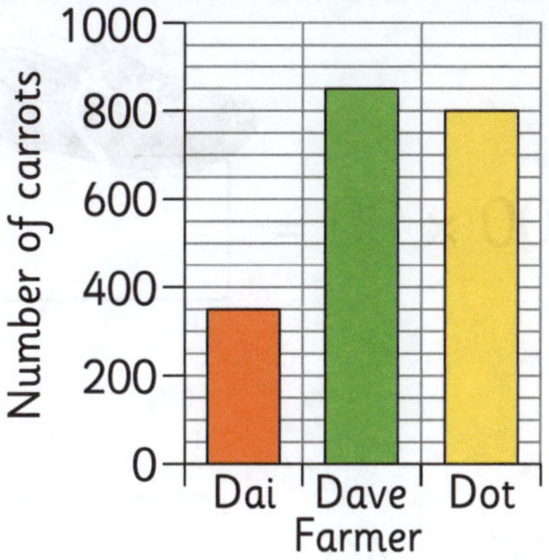

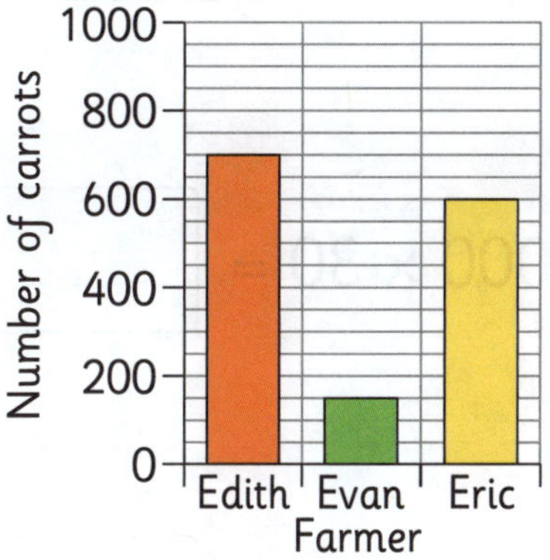

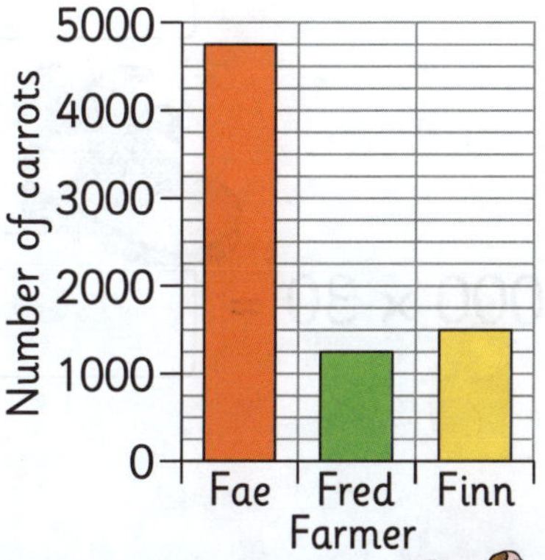

Today I scored ☐ out of 6.

# Week 11 — Day 2

Work out the answer to the multiplication.

4000 × 60 = 240 000

1) 300 × 30 =

2) 200 × 80 =

3) 500 × 40 =

4) 7000 × 30 =

5) 40 × 9000 =

6) 2000 × 30 =

7) 500 × 700 =

8) 400 × 60 =

9) 300 × 900 =

10) 300 × 700 =

11) 800 × 500 =

12) 9000 × 60 =

Today I scored [ ] out of 12.

# Week 11 — Day 3

Fill in the missing number to complete the equivalent fractions.

$\dfrac{3}{4} = \dfrac{\boxed{6}}{8}$

1) $\dfrac{2}{4} = \dfrac{\boxed{\phantom{0}}}{2}$

2) $\dfrac{1}{7} = \dfrac{\boxed{\phantom{0}}}{14}$

3) $\dfrac{1}{3} = \dfrac{\boxed{\phantom{0}}}{15}$

4) $\dfrac{1}{5} = \dfrac{\boxed{\phantom{0}}}{20}$

5) $\dfrac{4}{6} = \dfrac{\boxed{\phantom{0}}}{30}$

6) $\dfrac{1}{2} = \dfrac{5}{\boxed{\phantom{0}}}$

7) $\dfrac{3}{9} = \dfrac{\boxed{\phantom{0}}}{27}$

8) $\dfrac{3}{5} = \dfrac{18}{\boxed{\phantom{0}}}$

9) $\dfrac{6}{9} = \dfrac{2}{\boxed{\phantom{0}}}$

10) $\dfrac{10}{12} = \dfrac{50}{\boxed{\phantom{0}}}$

11) $\dfrac{3}{4} = \dfrac{\boxed{\phantom{0}}}{32}$

12) $\dfrac{4}{5} = \dfrac{28}{\boxed{\phantom{0}}}$

Today I scored ☐ out of 12.

# Week 11 — Day 4

Work out the answer to the division.

3500 ÷ 50 = 70

1) 1600 ÷ 40 =

2) 1800 ÷ 30 =

3) 2400 ÷ 60 =

4) 2800 ÷ 400 =

5) 36 000 ÷ 60 =

6) 27 000 ÷ 90 =

7) 32000 ÷ 800 =

8) 49000 ÷ 70 =

9) 72000 ÷ 600 =

10) 4500 ÷ 900 =

11) 54000 ÷ 60 =

12) 56000 ÷ 700 =

Today I scored ☐ out of 12.

# Week 11 — Day 5

Leon has the number of sweets shown. He splits them equally into the number of jars shown. Find the number of sweets in each jar, and the remainder.

7695 sweets

$$\begin{array}{r} 1\,2\,8\,2 \text{ r } 3 \\ 6\overline{)7\,^16\,^49\,^15} \end{array}$$

**1282** in each jar.

Remainder = **3**

**1** | 3669 sweets | 3

☐ in each jar.

Remainder = ☐

**4** | 8957 sweets | 4

☐ in each jar.

Remainder = ☐

**2** | 4835 sweets | 2

☐ in each jar.

Remainder = ☐

**5** | 7499 sweets | 7

☐ in each jar.

Remainder = ☐

**3** | 5865 sweets | 5

☐ in each jar.

Remainder = ☐

**6** | 6582 sweets | 9

☐ in each jar.

Remainder = ☐

Today I scored ☐ out of 6.

# Week 12 — Day 1

Mrs Crimble is cutting her delicious pies into sections. Circle the biggest section.

⟨ $\frac{11}{12}$ ⟩    $\frac{3}{4}$

1) $\frac{1}{10}$   $\frac{2}{5}$

2) $\frac{1}{3}$   $\frac{4}{6}$

3) $\frac{5}{8}$   $\frac{9}{16}$

4) $\frac{13}{28}$   $\frac{2}{4}$

5) $\frac{1}{27}$   $\frac{3}{9}$

6) $\frac{80}{100}$   $\frac{15}{20}$

7) $\frac{5}{16}$   $\frac{1}{4}$

8) $\frac{7}{10}$   $\frac{4}{5}$

9) $\frac{2}{11}$   $\frac{1}{44}$

10) $\frac{11}{12}$   $\frac{3}{4}$

11) $\frac{5}{14}$   $\frac{2}{7}$

12) $\frac{4}{9}$   $\frac{19}{45}$

Today I scored ☐ out of 12.

# Week 12 — Day 2

Sanjit is writing down some calculations. Use Sanjit's calculation to work out the missing symbol.

63 × 481 = 30303

30303 ÷ 481 = 63

① 41 × 555 = 22 755

22 755 ☐ 41 = 555

② 62 937 ÷ 999 = 63

63 ☐ 999 = 62 937

③ 3538 − 743 = 2795

743 ☐ 2795 = 3538

④ 78 × 627 = 48 906

48 906 ☐ 627 = 78

⑤ 52 448 ÷ 149 = 352

52 448 ☐ 352 = 149

⑥ 1484 − 891 = 593

1484 ☐ 593 = 891

⑦ 3493 × 46 = 160 678

160 678 ☐ 46 = 3493

⑧ 970 × 84 = 81 480

8148 ☐ 84 = 97

⑨ 27 280 ÷ 88 = 310

310 ☐ 880 = 272 800

⑩ 3696 ÷ 112 = 33

33 ☐ 11.2 = 369.6

Today I scored ☐ out of 10.

# Week 12 — Day 4

Sammy the builder is designing some new sheds. Find the perimeter of the shaded area on each plan.

3.3 m, 2 m → **10.6 m**

1) 1.8 m, 2.4 m → ___ m

2) 1.7 m, 4.6 m → ___ m

3) 3.85 m, 2.95 m → ___ m

4) 3.49 m, 1.23 m → ___ m

5) 2.3 m, 1.3 m, 2.3 m, 1.3 m → ___ m

6) 1.24 m, 1.24 m, 2.48 m, 1.24 m → ___ m

Today I scored ___ out of 6.

# Week 12 — Day 5

Work out how many flowers are not red or blue.

Jess has 100 flowers. If $\frac{1}{2}$ of her flowers are red and $\frac{1}{4}$ are blue, how many flowers are not red or blue?

25

1) Ari has 40 flowers. If $\frac{1}{4}$ of his flowers are red and $\frac{1}{2}$ are blue, how many flowers are not red or blue?

2) Sally has 30 flowers. If $\frac{1}{3}$ of her flowers are red and $\frac{1}{3}$ are blue, how many flowers are not red or blue?

3) Tim has 120 flowers. If $\frac{1}{3}$ of his flowers are red and $\frac{1}{6}$ are blue, how many flowers are not red or blue?

4) Izzy has 81 flowers. If $\frac{1}{3}$ of her flowers are red and $\frac{1}{9}$ are blue, how many flowers are not red or blue?

5) Rico has 144 flowers. If $\frac{1}{6}$ of his flowers are red and $\frac{1}{12}$ are blue, how many flowers are not red or blue?

6) Si has 88 flowers. If $\frac{1}{11}$ of his flowers are red and $\frac{1}{4}$ are blue, how many flowers are not red or blue?

Today I scored ☐ out of 6.

# Answers

## Week 1 — Day 1

1. 189
2. 312
3. 385
4. 821
5. 259
6. 7263
7. 6702
8. 2192
9. 5043
10. 1389
11. 1335
12. 7289

## Week 1 — Day 2

1. 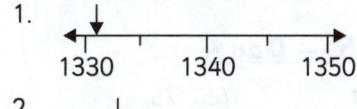 (1330, 1340, 1350)
2. (1640, 1660, 1680)
3. 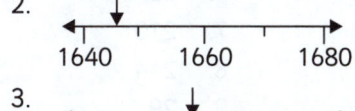 (780, 790)
4. (500, 550, 600)
5. (1890, 1900, 1910)
6. 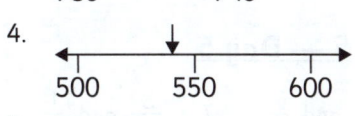 (2510, 2515, 2520)
7. (7005, 7010, 7015, 7020)
8. (2025, 2050, 2075)

## Week 1 — Day 3

1. 582 cm
2. 7.6 m
3. 0.7 m
4. 15.2 m
5. 19 m
6. 2322 cm
7. 117 cm
8. 361 cm
9. 20.03 m
10. 1119 cm

## Week 1 — Day 4

1. 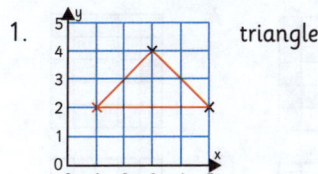 triangle
2. square
3. 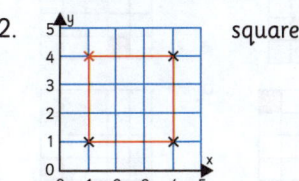 kite
4. 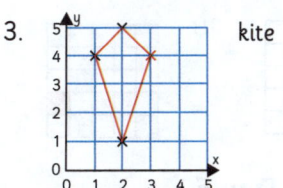 pentagon
5. 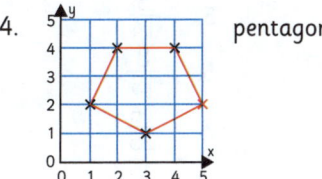 hexagon
6. 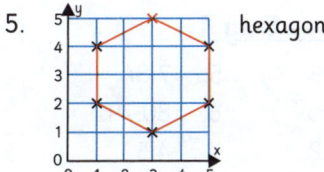 
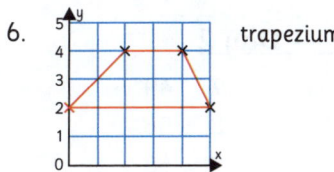 trapezium

## Week 1 — Day 5

1. £14.70
2. £6.30
3. £15.60
4. £14.30
5. £14.50
6. £16.80
7. £12.20
8. £9.40

## Week 2 — Day 1

1. 53
2. 96
3. 84
4. 39
5. 61
6. 9

## Week 2 — Day 2

1. 1368
2. 3542
3. 1576
4. 1737
5. 4884
6. 4428
7. 1284
8. 3942
9. 2585
10. 6075

## Week 2 — Day 3

1. 50
2. 110
3. 30
4. 412
5. 60
6. 90
7. 110
8. 40
9. 101
10. 70
11. 30
12. 90

## Week 2 — Day 4

1. 15
2. 5
3. 10
4. 25
5. 20
6. 18

## Week 2 — Day 5

1. 3
2. 2
3. 3
4. 4
5. 3
6. 5
7. 4
8. 4
9. 9
10. 11
11. 8
12. 12

## Week 3 — Day 1

1. 4, 10, **16, 22, 28, 34**
2. 109, 129, **149, 169, 189, 209**
3. 56, 49, **42, 35, 28, 21**
4. 4321, 5321, **6321, 7321, 8321, 9321**
5. 42, 51, **60, 69, 78, 87**
6. 1223, 1373, **1523, 1673, 1823, 1973**
7. 682, 657, **632, 607, 582, 557**
8. 410, 485, **560, 635, 710, 785**

## Week 3 — Day 2

1. 20 m
2. 22 m
3. 14 m
4. 18 m
5. 16 m
6. 18 m
7. 18 m
8. 16 m
9. 18 m
10. 26 m

## Week 3 — Day 3
1. 7 + 6
2. 13 + 3
3. 4 + 17
4. 3 + 9
5. 22 + 19
6. 21 + 1
7. 11 + 6
8. 11 + 1
9. 10 + 9
10. 5 + 6

## Week 3 — Day 4
1. 16:11
2. 12:22
3. 19:07
4. 09:39
5. 14:27
6. 20:51
7. 11:19
8. 13:08
9. 18:50
10. 15:55

## Week 3 — Day 5
1. 75 cm
2. 120 cm
3. 240 cm
4. 40 cm
5. 240 cm
6. 160 cm
7. 175 cm
8. 150 cm

## Week 4 — Day 1
1. 81 604
2. 102 341
3. 720 466
4. 354 071
5. 30 016
6. 211 509
7. 905 613
8. 690 850

## Week 4 — Day 2
1. 10 502, **11 502**, **12 502**, **13 502**, **14 502**
2. 42 357, **42 257**, **42 157**, **42 057**, **41 957**
3. 281 650, **291 650**, **301 650**, **311 650**, **321 650**
4. 50 710, **50 810**, **50 910**, **51 010**, **51 110**
5. 491 081, **391 081**, **291 081**, **191 081**, **91 081**
6. 40 023, **30 023**, **20 023**, **10 023**, **23**

## Week 4 — Day 3
1. 5774, 5836, 6098, 6123
2. 94 951, 98 407, 108 328, 110 622
3. 37 053, 37 590, 37 615, 37 712
4. 204 691, 204 836, 205 674, 205 720
5. 570 650, 570 885, 572 862, 572 872
6. 433 892, 433 913, 433 919, 434 008

## Week 4 — Day 4

1.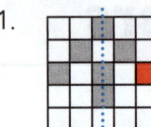
2.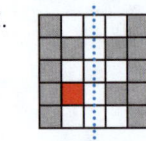
3.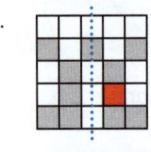
4.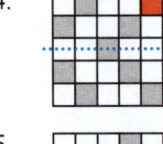
5. 
6.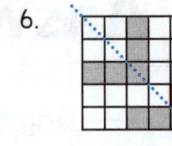
7. 
8. 
9.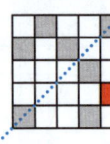
10. 

## Week 4 — Day 5
1. $\frac{3}{4}$
2. $\frac{1}{6}$
3. $\frac{2}{5}$
4. $\frac{5}{9}$
5. $\frac{5}{14}$
6. $\frac{8}{13}$
7. $\frac{16}{25}$
8. $\frac{9}{36}$ or $\frac{1}{4}$

## Week 5 — Day 1
1. 46 825
2. 65 200
3. 75 058
4. 88 538
5. 7.84
6. 80.79
7. 4.51
8. 37.58

## Week 5 — Day 2
1. 36
2. 65
3. 70
4. 24
5. 81
6. 72
7. 49
8. 96
9. 66
10. 96
11. 80
12. 75

## Week 5 — Day 3
1. 9: ①× 9, ③× 3
   12: ①× 12, 2 × 6, ③× 4
2. 6: ①×⑥ ②×③
   18: ①× 18, ②× 9, ③×⑥
3. 5: ①×⑤
   30: ①× 30, 2 × 15, 3 × 10, 6 ×⑤
4. 10: ①× 10, 2 ×⑤
   45: ①× 45, 3 × 15, ⑤× 9
5. 4: ①×④ ②×②
   24: ①× 24, ②× 12, 3 × 8, ④× 6
6. 21: ①× 21, ③× 7
   36: ①× 36, 2 × 18, ③× 12, 4 × 9, 6 × 6

## Week 5 — Day 4
1. 240
2. 300
3. 48
4. 36
5. 56
6. 75
7. 210
8. 244
9. 29
10. 45

## Week 5 — Day 5
1. $\frac{4}{10}$ and $\frac{2}{5}$
2. $\frac{3}{4}$ and $\frac{75}{100}$
3. $\frac{1}{3}$ and $\frac{2}{6}$
4. $\frac{5}{20}$ and $\frac{1}{4}$
5. $\frac{6}{10}$ and $\frac{3}{5}$
6. $\frac{10}{20}$ and $\frac{1}{2}$
7. $\frac{3}{12}$ and $\frac{1}{4}$
8. $\frac{14}{20}$ and $\frac{7}{10}$
9. $\frac{5}{6}$ and $\frac{10}{12}$
10. $\frac{16}{20}$ and $\frac{4}{5}$
11. $\frac{5}{15}$ and $\frac{1}{3}$
12. $\frac{40}{100}$ and $\frac{2}{5}$

## Week 6 — Day 1
1. A: (3, 3)  B: (2, 1)
2. A: (1, 4)  B: (1, 2)
3. A: (5, 2)  B: (2, 3)
4. A: (2, 0)  B: (4, 4)
5. A: (1, 5)  B: (4, 3)
6. A: (5, 5)  B: (3, 4)

## Week 6 — Day 2
1. 4534
2. 1531
3. 81 112
4. 40 213
5. 23 126
6. 24 918
7. 33 062
8. 18 507

## Week 6 — Day 3
1. 20 cm
2. 45 kg
3. 12.5 m
4. 63 mm
5. 20 g
6. 7.5 km
7. 75 ml
8. 100 l

### Week 6 — Day 4
1. 42.7
2. 30.9
3. 9.09
4. 52.88
5. 30.31
6. 84.69
7. 23.37
8. 43.94

### Week 6 — Day 5
1. 200 + 700 = 900 ✓
2. 500 − 300 = 200 ✗
3. 6000 + 8000 = 14 000 ✗
4. 9000 − 800 = 8200 ✓
5. 4 + 2 = 6 ✓
6. 14 − 6 = 8 ✓
7. 8 + 6 = 14 ✗
8. 40 − 28 = 12 ✓
9. 55 + 70 = 125 ✗
10. 103 + 67 = 170 ✓
11. 18 − 13 = 5 ✓
12. 108 − 10 = 98 ✗

### Week 7 — Day 1
1. 3500
2. 6800
3. 43 400
4. 51 600
5. 34 400
6. 40 300
7. 16 100
8. 56 000
9. 9500
10. 15 400
11. 94 200
12. 56 600

### Week 7 — Day 2

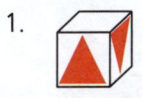  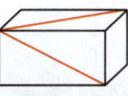

### Week 7 — Day 3
1. £4.49
2. £6.50
3. 90p
4. £1.35
5. 99p
6. £1.25
7. £2.10
8. £1.49

### Week 7 — Day 4
1. 4
2. 2
3. 12
4. 5
5. 6
6. 3
7. 4
8. 8
9. 16
10. 8
11. 15
12. 12

### Week 7 — Day 5

1.

| Colour | Number of cars | Total |
|---|---|---|
| Blue | ●● | **10** |
| Black | ●●● | 15 |
| Purple | ●●●●● | 25 |

2.

| Colour | Number of cars | Total |
|---|---|---|
| Gold | ●●●●● | **9** |
| Silver | ●◗ | 3 |
| Bronze | ●●●● | 8 |

3.

| Colour | Number of cars | Total |
|---|---|---|
| Red | ●●● | 9 |
| Green | ●● | 6 |
| Pink | ●●●● | **12** |

4.

| Colour | Number of cars | Total |
|---|---|---|
| Grey | ● | 10 |
| Beige | ●●◗ | **25** |
| Cream | ●●●●◗ | 45 |

5.

| Colour | Number of cars | Total |
|---|---|---|
| Brown | ●●●●● | 40 |
| Yellow | ●●●◗ | **26** |
| Green | ●◗ | 12 |

6. Key: ● = 4 cars

| Colour | Number of cars | Total |
|---|---|---|
| Blue | ●●●●● | 20 |
| Pink | ●◗ | **10** |
| Black | ●●●● | 16 |

### Week 8 — Day 1
1. $\frac{17}{100}$
2. $\frac{66}{100}$
3. $\frac{9}{100}$
4. $\frac{25}{100}$
5. $\frac{44}{100}$
6. $\frac{36}{100}$
7. $\frac{1}{100}$
8. $\frac{10}{100}$
9. $\frac{8}{100}$
10. $\frac{99}{100}$
11. $\frac{40}{100}$
12. $\frac{70}{100}$

### Week 8 — Day 2
1. 70
2. 12
3. 4560
4. 9
5. 55 000
6. 37.1
7. 43.8
8. 0.22
9. 891
10. 77.85
11. 3460
12. 0.334

### Week 8 — Day 3

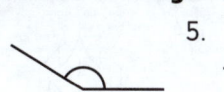
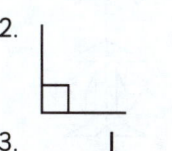 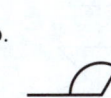
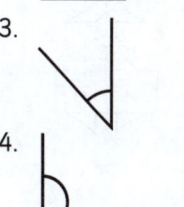 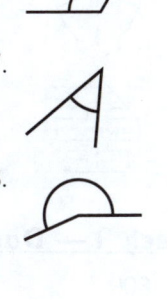

### Week 8 — Day 4
1. Leah: 18  Wade: 9
2. Leah: 66  Wade: 33
3. Leah: 34  Wade: 17
4. Leah: 76  Wade: 38
5. Leah: 154  Wade: 77
6. Leah: 216  Wade: 108
7. Leah: 294  Wade: 147
8. Leah: 550  Wade: 275

### Week 8 — Day 5
1. 100
2. 84
3. 35
4. 1000
5. 37 350
6. 1000
7. 10
8. 7.3
9. 100
10. 100
11. 400
12. 330

### Week 9 — Day 1
1. 90
2. 340
3. 3660
4. 100
5. 600
6. 1000
7. 7000
8. 1 000 000
9. 65 000
10. 50 000
11. 100 000
12. 320 000

### Week 9 — Day 2
1. 21 600
2. 19 640
3. 26 635
4. 76 096
5. 14 630
6. 23 892
7. 16 136
8. 89 919

### Week 9 — Day 3
1. over
2. under
3. under
4. over
5. over
6. over
7. under
8. under
9. over
10. under

## 64

### Week 9 — Day 4

1.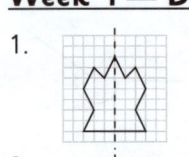
2.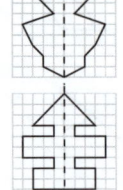
3. 
4.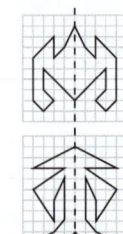
5.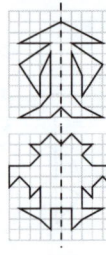
6. 

### Week 9 — Day 5

1. 800
2. 245
3. 240
4. 50
5. 390
6. 564
7. 7000
8. 70

### Week 10 — Day 1

1. 45°
2. 100°
3. 30°
4. 150°
5. 250°
6. 190°
7. 320°
8. 290°

### Week 10 — Day 2

1. 735
2. 3120
3. 2460
4. 2350
5. 2200
6. 1545
7. 6660
8. 4905
9. 3360
10. 20 100

### Week 10 — Day 3

1. VII
2. XIV
3. XXII
4. L
5. C
6. LVI
7. XXXIII
8. LXVII
9. XIX
10. XLIX
11. LXXXIV
12. XCIX

### Week 10 — Day 4

For Q1-8 below, allow any answer in the range given.

1. 58-62°
2. 18-22°
3. 41-45°
4. 65-69°
5. 29-33°
6. 14-18°
7. 83-87°
8. 133-137°

### Week 10 — Day 5

1. 30°
2. 80°
3. 21°
4. 120°
5. 150°
6. 169°
7. 250°
8. 340°

### Week 11 — Day 1

1. 400
2. 200
3. 2800
4. 500
5. 550
6. 3500

### Week 11 — Day 2

1. 9000
2. 16 000
3. 20 000
4. 210 000
5. 360 000
6. 60 000
7. 350 000
8. 24 000
9. 270 000
10. 210 000
11. 400 000
12. 540 000

### Week 11 — Day 3

1. $\frac{1}{2}$
2. $\frac{2}{14}$
3. $\frac{5}{15}$
4. $\frac{4}{20}$
5. $\frac{20}{30}$
6. $\frac{5}{10}$
7. $\frac{9}{27}$
8. $\frac{18}{30}$
9. $\frac{2}{3}$
10. $\frac{50}{60}$
11. $\frac{24}{32}$
12. $\frac{28}{35}$

### Week 11 — Day 4

1. 40
2. 60
3. 40
4. 7
5. 600
6. 300
7. 40
8. 700
9. 120
10. 5
11. 900
12. 80

### Week 11 — Day 5

1. 1223 in each jar. Remainder = 0
2. 2417 in each jar. Remainder = 1
3. 1173 in each jar. Remainder = 0
4. 2239 in each jar. Remainder = 1
5. 1071 in each jar. Remainder = 2
6. 731 in each jar. Remainder = 3

### Week 12 — Day 1

1. $\frac{2}{5}$
2. $\frac{4}{6}$
3. $\frac{5}{8}$
4. $\frac{2}{4}$
5. $\frac{3}{9}$
6. $\frac{80}{100}$
7. $\frac{5}{16}$
8. $\frac{4}{5}$
9. $\frac{2}{11}$
10. $\frac{11}{12}$
11. $\frac{5}{14}$
12. $\frac{4}{9}$

### Week 12 — Day 2

1. ÷
2. ×
3. +
4. ÷
5. ÷
6. −
7. ÷
8. ÷
9. ×
10. ×

### Week 12 — Day 3

1. $\frac{1}{2}$
2. $\frac{2}{5}$
3. $\frac{1}{5}$
4. $\frac{3}{8}$
5. $\frac{7}{9}$
6. $\frac{3}{7}$
7. $\frac{7}{15}$
8. $\frac{5}{8}$

### Week 12 — Day 4

1. 8.4 m
2. 12.6 m
3. 13.6 m
4. 9.44 m
5. 14.4 m
6. 12.4 m

### Week 12 — Day 5

1. 10
2. 10
3. 60
4. 45
5. 108
6. 58